PRACTICAL
REGULATION
COMMERCIAL PILOT 2022

PRACTICAL REGULATION

COMMERCIAL PILOT 2022

Selections from Titles 14 and 49
of the Code of Federal Regulations

Created By Benjamin Samples & Casey Rice

Published by Patch Aero LLC

PATCH AERO

PRACTICAL REGULATION Commercial Pilot 2022

This publication contains current regulations as of October 2021. It is designed as a study aid to familiarize aviators with pertinent regulations for their certificate level, category, and class. None of the material in this publication supersedes any documents, procedures, or regulations issued by the Federal Aviation Administration, the Department of Transportation, or any other agency. Changes and updates to regulation should be regularly reviewed at the following websites:

> https://www.faa.gov/regulations_policies/faa_regulations/
> https://ecfr.gov/

Patch Aero LLC
Boca Raton, FL
www.patchaero.com

All rights reserved. Cover design and layout provided by Benjamin Samples.

ISBN   978-1-7379549-1-0
LCCN   2021921346

Printed in the United States of America.

9 8 7 6 5 4 3 2 1 0

Introduction

I've found myself in a constant search for understanding within our world of aviation. This search has connected me with a brotherhood of fellow aviators. Knowing something and being sure of it—especially considering the dire consequences we face if we're wrong—has become somewhat of my obsession. It's like there's an itch that's just out of reach. And unfortunately, there's so much "knowledge" out there that is ultimately sort of unreliable. As aviators dig into their understanding of one regulation, they uncover three more that need further analysis. Regulation is not designed to be a roadblock to the enjoyment of flight, but rather a foundation for safe and reliable operation.

Like most aviators, I often find myself attempting to connect my daily life experiences into lessons that are applicable to things in flying—it's a way to take what is known and connect it to what is yet known so that I can refine my network of knowledge. I recently had the fortunate opportunity to talk with a master brewer at a local brew house. He said, "it's easy to make a good beer once; the art is in making the same beer over and over and making it taste the same every time." There is a similar approach that sort of applies with the Federal Aviation Administration and their regulations. They are designed to make the process of flight safe and repeatable, over and over and over again. The fact that today's flight ended safely cannot rely on luck. The pathway to continued safe flight is supported by regulations designed to keep us safe and make that act repeatable, flight after flight after flight.

If we examine regulations through the eyes of the brew master, we may consider them an art of ensuring repeatable, safe outcomes. Uncovering and understanding regulation unlocks more tools for use at our disposal. A continual pursuit of understanding keeps us always engaged and always learning. Trying to understand regulation is an obviously daunting task, especially if you examine them by trying to learn and understand every one ever written all at once—or in the case of the brew master, understanding every recipe ever made. Instead, take it one regulation at a time and build a safe and solid foundation. Fly safe and always reach for the itch of understanding.

The *Practical Regulation* Network

READ THIS SECTION FIRST!!!

Note: this will be on the test!

The Code of Federal Regulations spans volumes and volumes—in print, it'd easily fill any room to the ceiling. And regulations change all the time. The minute we put them into print, they are essentially out of date.

Moreover, **regulations ultimately comprise a network, not a list**.

Probably the best way for us aviators to grasp regulation is to start getting familiar with the network—the topics, rationale, relationships, and scenarios they represent—rather than rotely memorizing facts and figures.

As you can see from the size of *Practical Regulation*, it isn't a traditional FAR/AIM like those thick compilations produced by several (awesome) publishers like ASA or Jeppesen. Neither is *Practical Regulation* necessarily meant to be read from front to back (although you are welcome to do so). As you go through your training, your instructors or peers will relate information to you about various topics and regulations, encouraging you to look them up. As you view the material, you will naturally begin to summarize and internalize the logic of particular regulations. Over time, you will gradually see connections between them and relate each to others—this is the foundation of your network. Over more time, you will re-read regulations and refine your understanding of specific words and phrasing that you formerly glossed over—this is the strength of your network. As you progress through certificates and ratings, you will also understand regulations from different perspectives, such as from a training pilot's needs or from an instructor's needs—this is the wisdom of your network. This sort of differentiation forms a living and evolving framework of understanding that will support you throughout your flying career—even as regulations change, as the industry changes, and as you advance.

In *Practical Regulation*, we compile the regulations applicable to your certificate level, aircraft category, and class. We present in suitable outline spacing and indentation to provide better cognitive grouping of topics. This grouping supports the construction of your network.

Because so much peripheral information is interwoven into each outline level, we also summarize and *italicize* non-pertinent topics. These usually refer to other categories of aircraft or other regulatory parts (like airline operations or on-demand charters, for example). **So, if you see portions italicized, keep in mind that we have summarized or otherwise redacted those regulatory sections to maintain clarity and conciseness**; if you want to learn more about those supplementary sections, feel free to check them out online at the following websites:

https://www.faa.gov/regulations_policies/faa_regulations/

https://ecfr.gov/

We encourage marking up your copy of *Practical Regulation* by notating the connections you find between regulations—make it your own! While we could provide so many of these relationships, the creation of your own network requires you to come to these realizations through instruction and exploration; if we simply referenced them for you, they'd simply be another entry in your "list" of rotely memorized facts. Additionally, when you see words like, "except as provided by 61.110," follow the rationale out through the network of regulations to see the logic of the exception—sometimes they are applicable to your current network and sometimes they are not.

Highlighting

The process of highlighting is also a useful technique in blocking out your network. However, simply grabbing your favorite color and painting away simply results in pile of memorized lines—another "list." Instead, your highlighting process should have a rationale that supports a "network."

One such process we have seen successful students apply uses at least three colors to identify and relate types of information that effectively become nodes in the network.

Yellow is perhaps reserved for titles. By highlighting pertinent titles, you are able to visualize the size of a given block of regulation that *should be* related by seeing the yellow title above it and the yellow title of the next section below it.

Green is might be reserved for definitions or requirements. These may relate to actions you need to take or steps you must satisfy enroute to your objectives or in exercise of your privileges—like the fact that you need to perform a preflight inspection.

Blue is may be reserved for rote memory items, limits, transients, or particular values. While the network grows and branches out, there are still hard numbers that must be included in your framework. These may be facts that just need memorized—e.g., the distance of a cross country flight or an altitude you must fly in a given direction.

Again, highlighting is not meant to prove to your instructor you read through the regulations—it is meant to support your network. Anytime you find yourself highlighting more than about four lines of text, ask yourself if that entire selection really strengthens your network. If not, don't highlight it all; if so, it's probably better to simply highlight a box around that given section and summarize it in your own words in the margin or foot note. There are no extra points for how many highlighters you go through in the process.

Tabbing

Some successful flyers also like tabbing their regulations, which can be an efficient way to quickly find something in your network. However, you should rely on tabbing to remind you of where things are in your network, not of what topics and regulations are actually held within it. For example, a tab should help you find 61.56 quickly, not remind you that there is such a thing as a "flight review" when the examiner asks if you can act as PIC next November.

Good Enough is not Enough

Practical Regulation can be used throughout your training, your stage checks, your practical tests, and your overall progression as an aviator. Again, as you develop your network of what regulation is all about, use *Practical Regulation* as a pocket guide to refer to during class, at the flight school, or when the weather has you socked in. And yes, these regulations will come up on your practical test. They will also come up on your written tests, your flight review, discussions at your first and second and next flying jobs...

But the real reason we want to ingest regulation is to be able to safely operate with our peers and friends in the industry; as we're zipping through the air in three dimensions, it is our responsibility to make sure we never take advantage of the exceptional privileges we share as aviators and that we also seek a higher standard than "good enough."

Table of Contents

Title 14 CFR, Part 1

Definitions and Abbreviations

§ 1.1 General definitions.

As used in Subchapters A through K of this chapter, unless the context requires otherwise:

Administrator means the Federal Aviation Administrator or any person to whom he has delegated his authority in the matter concerned.

Aerodynamic coefficients means non-dimensional coefficients for aerodynamic forces and moments.

Air carrier means a person who undertakes directly by lease, or other arrangement, to engage in air transportation.

Air commerce means interstate, overseas, or foreign air commerce or the transportation of mail by aircraft or any operation or navigation of aircraft within the limits of any Federal airway or any operation or navigation of aircraft which directly affects, or which may endanger safety in, interstate, overseas, or foreign air commerce.

Aircraft means a device that is used or intended to be used for flight in the air.

Aircraft engine means an engine that is used or intended to be used for propelling aircraft. It includes turbosuperchargers, appurtenances, and accessories necessary for its functioning, but does not include propellers.

Airframe means the fuselage, booms, nacelles, cowlings, fairings, airfoil surfaces (including rotors but excluding propellers and rotating airfoils of engines), and landing gear of an aircraft and their accessories and controls.

Airplane means an engine-driven fixed-wing aircraft heavier than air, that is supported in flight by the dynamic reaction of the air against its wings.

Airport means an area of land or water that is used or intended to be used for the landing and takeoff of aircraft, and includes its buildings and facilities, if any.

Air traffic means aircraft operating in the air or on an airport surface, exclusive of loading ramps and parking areas.

Air traffic *clearance* means an authorization by air traffic control, for the purpose of preventing collision between known aircraft, for an aircraft to proceed under specified traffic conditions within controlled airspace.

Air traffic *control* means a service operated by appropriate authority to promote the safe, orderly, and expeditious flow of air traffic.

Air Traffic Service (ATS) route is a specified route designated for channeling the flow of traffic as necessary for the provision of air traffic services. The term "ATS route" refers to a variety of airways, including jet routes, area navigation (RNAV) routes, and arrival and departure routes. An ATS route is defined by route specifications, which may include:

1) An ATS route designator;

2) The path to or from significant points;

3) Distance between significant points;

4) Reporting requirements; and

5) The lowest safe altitude determined by the appropriate authority.

Air transportation means interstate, overseas, or foreign air transportation or the transportation of mail by aircraft.

Alert Area. An alert area is established to inform pilots of a specific area wherein a high volume of pilot training or an unusual type of aeronautical activity is conducted.

Alternate airport means an airport at which an aircraft may land if a landing at the intended airport becomes inadvisable.

Altitude engine means a reciprocating aircraft engine having a rated takeoff power that is producible from sea level to an established higher altitude.

Appliance means any instrument, mechanism, equipment, part, apparatus, appurtenance, or accessory, including communications equipment, that is used or intended to be used in operating or controlling an aircraft in flight, is installed in or attached to the aircraft, and is not part of an airframe, engine, or propeller.

Approved, unless used with reference to another person, means approved by the FAA or any person to whom the FAA has delegated its authority in the matter concerned, or approved under the provisions of a bilateral agreement between the United States and a foreign country or jurisdiction.

Area navigation (RNAV) is a method of navigation that permits aircraft operations on any desired flight path.

Area navigation (RNAV) *route* is an ATS route based on RNAV that can be used by suitably equipped aircraft.

Brake horsepower means the power delivered at the propeller shaft (main drive or main output) of an aircraft engine.

Calibrated airspeed means the indicated airspeed of an aircraft, corrected for position and instrument error. Calibrated airspeed is equal to true airspeed in standard atmosphere at sea level.

Canard means the forward wing of a canard configuration and may be a fixed, movable, or variable geometry surface, with or without control surfaces.

Canard configuration means a configuration in which the span of the forward wing is substantially less than that of the main wing.

Category:

1) As used with respect to the certification, ratings, privileges, and limitations of airmen, means a broad classification of aircraft. Examples include: airplane; rotorcraft; glider; and lighter-than-air; and

2) As used with respect to the certification of aircraft, means a grouping of aircraft based upon intended use or operating limitations. Examples include: transport, normal, utility, acrobatic, limited, restricted, and provisional.

Category II operation, with respect to the operation of aircraft, means a straight-in ILS approach to the runway of an airport under a Category

II ILS instrument approach procedure issued by the Administrator or other appropriate authority.

Category III operations, with respect to the operation of aircraft, means an ILS approach to, and landing on, the runway of an airport using a Category III ILS instrument approach procedure issued by the Administrator or other appropriate authority.

Ceiling means the height above the earth's surface of the lowest layer of clouds or obscuring phenomena that is reported as "broken", "overcast", or "obscuration", and not classified as "thin" or "partial".

Civil aircraft means aircraft other than public aircraft.

Class:

1) As used with respect to the certification, ratings, privileges, and limitations of airmen, means a classification of aircraft within a category having similar operating characteristics. Examples include: single engine; multiengine; land; water; gyroplane; helicopter; airship; and free balloon; and

2) As used with respect to the certification of aircraft, means a broad grouping of aircraft having similar characteristics of propulsion, flight, or landing. Examples include: airplane; rotorcraft; glider; balloon; landplane; and seaplane.

Clearway means:

1) For turbine engine powered airplanes certificated after August 29, 1959, an area beyond the runway, not less than 500 feet wide, centrally located about the extended centerline of the runway, and under the control of the airport authorities. The clearway is expressed in terms of a clearway plane, extending from the end of the runway with an upward slope not exceeding 1.25 percent, above which no object nor any terrain protrudes. However, threshold lights may protrude above the plane if their height above the end of the runway is 26 inches or less and if they are located to each side of the runway.

2) For turbine engine powered airplanes certificated after September 30, 1958, but before August 30, 1959, an area beyond the takeoff

runway extending no less than 300 feet on either side of the extended centerline of the runway, at an elevation no higher than the elevation of the end of the runway, clear of all fixed obstacles, and under the control of the airport authorities.

Commercial operator means a person who, for compensation or hire, engages in the carriage by aircraft in air commerce of persons or property, other than as an air carrier or foreign air carrier or under the authority of Part 375 of this title. Where it is doubtful that an operation is for "compensation or hire", the test applied is whether the carriage by air is merely incidental to the person's other business or is, in itself, a major enterprise for profit.

Controlled airspace means an airspace of defined dimensions within which air traffic control service is provided to IFR flights and to VFR flights in accordance with the airspace classification.

Note: Controlled airspace is a generic term that covers Class A, Class B, Class C, Class D, and Class E airspace.

Controlled Firing Area. A controlled firing area is established to contain activities, which if not conducted in a controlled environment, would be hazardous to nonparticipating aircraft.

Crewmember means a person assigned to perform duty in an aircraft during flight time.

Critical engine means the engine whose failure would most adversely affect the performance or handling qualities of an aircraft.

Decision altitude (DA) is a specified altitude in an instrument approach procedure at which the pilot must decide whether to initiate an immediate missed approach if the pilot does not see the required visual reference, or to continue the approach. Decision altitude is expressed in feet above mean sea level.

Decision height (DH) is a specified height above the ground in an instrument approach procedure at which the pilot must decide whether to initiate an immediate missed approach if the pilot does not see the required visual reference, or to continue the approach. Decision height is expressed in feet above ground level.

Early ETOPS means ETOPS type design approval obtained without gaining non-ETOPS service experience on the candidate airplane-engine combination certified for ETOPS.

EFVS operation means an operation in which visibility conditions require an EFVS to be used in lieu of natural vision to perform an approach or landing, determine enhanced flight visibility, identify required visual references, or conduct a rollout.

Enhanced flight visibility (EFV) means the average forward horizontal distance, from the cockpit of an aircraft in flight, at which prominent topographical objects may be clearly distinguished and identified by day or night by a pilot using an enhanced flight vision system.

Enhanced flight vision system (EFVS) means an installed aircraft system which uses an electronic means to provide a display of the forward external scene topography (the natural or manmade features of a place or region especially in a way to show their relative positions and elevation) through the use of imaging sensors, including but not limited to forward-looking infrared, millimeter wave radiometry, millimeter wave radar, or low-light level image intensification. An EFVS includes the display element, sensors, computers and power supplies, indications, and controls.

Equivalent airspeed means the calibrated airspeed of an aircraft corrected for adiabatic compressible flow for the particular altitude. Equivalent airspeed is equal to calibrated airspeed in standard atmosphere at sea level.

ETOPS Significant System means an airplane system, including the propulsion system, the failure or malfunctioning of which could adversely affect the safety of an ETOPS flight, or the continued safe flight and landing of an airplane during an ETOPS diversion. Each ETOPS significant system is either an ETOPS group 1 significant system or an ETOPS group 2 significant system.

1) An ETOPS group 1 Significant System–

i) Has fail-safe characteristics directly linked to the degree of redundancy provided by the number of engines on the airplane.

ii) Is a system, the failure or malfunction of which could result in an IFSD, loss of thrust control, or other power loss.

iii) Contributes significantly to the safety of an ETOPS diversion by providing additional redundancy for any system power source lost as a result of an inoperative engine.

iv) Is essential for prolonged operation of an airplane at engine inoperative altitudes.

2) An ETOPS group 2 significant system is an ETOPS significant system that is not an ETOPS group 1 significant system.

Extended Operations (ETOPS) means an airplane flight operation, other than an all-cargo operation in an airplane with more than two engines, during which a portion of the flight is conducted beyond a time threshold identified in part 121 or part 135 of this chapter that is determined using an approved one-engine-inoperative cruise speed under standard atmospheric conditions in still air.

Extended over-water operation means–

1) With respect to aircraft other than helicopters, an operation over water at a horizontal distance of more than 50 nautical miles from the nearest shoreline; and

2) With respect to helicopters, an operation over water at a horizontal distance of more than 50 nautical miles from the nearest shoreline and more than 50 nautical miles from an off-shore heliport structure.

Final approach fix (FAF) defines the beginning of the final approach segment and the point where final segment descent may begin.

Final takeoff speed means the speed of the airplane that exists at the end of the takeoff path in the en route configuration with one engine inoperative.

Fireproof–

1) With respect to materials and parts used to confine fire in a designated fire zone, means the capacity to withstand at least as well as steel in dimensions appropriate for the purpose for which they are used, the heat produced when there is a severe fire of extended duration in that zone; and

2) With respect to other materials and parts, means the capacity to withstand the heat associated with fire at least as well as steel in dimensions appropriate for the purpose for which they are used.

Fire resistant–

1) With respect to sheet or structural members means the capacity to withstand the heat associated with fire at least as well as aluminum alloy in dimensions appropriate for the purpose for which they are used; and

2) With respect to fluid-carrying lines, fluid system parts, wiring, air ducts, fittings, and powerplant controls, means the capacity to perform the intended functions under the heat and other conditions likely to occur when there is a fire at the place concerned.

Flame resistant means not susceptible to combustion to the point of propagating a flame, beyond safe limits, after the ignition source is removed.

Flammable, with respect to a fluid or gas, means susceptible to igniting readily or to exploding.

Flap extended speed means the highest speed permissible with wing flaps in a prescribed extended position.

Flash resistant means not susceptible to burning violently when ignited.

Flightcrew member means a pilot, flight engineer, or flight navigator assigned to duty in an aircraft during flight time.

Flight level means a level of constant atmospheric pressure related to a reference datum of 29.92 inches of mercury. Each is stated in three digits that represent hundreds of feet. For example, flight level 250 represents a barometric altimeter indication of 25,000 feet; flight level 255, an indication of 25,500 feet.

Flight plan means specified information, relating to the intended flight of an aircraft, that is filed orally or in writing with air traffic control.

Flight simulation training device (FSTD) means a full flight simulator or a flight training device.

Flight time means:

1) Pilot time that commences when an aircraft moves under its own power for the purpose of flight and ends when the aircraft comes to rest after landing; or

2) For a glider without self-launch capability, pilot time that commences when the glider is towed for the purpose of flight and ends when the glider comes to rest after landing.

Flight training device (FTD) means a replica of aircraft instruments, equipment, panels, and controls in an open flight deck area or an enclosed aircraft cockpit replica. It includes the equipment and computer programs necessary to represent aircraft (or set of aircraft) operations in ground and flight conditions having the full range of capabilities of the systems installed in the device as described in part 60 of this chapter and the qualification performance standard (QPS) for a specific FTD qualification level.

Flight visibility means the average forward horizontal distance, from the cockpit of an aircraft in flight, at which prominent unlighted objects may be seen and identified by day and prominent lighted objects may be seen and identified by night.

Foreign air carrier means any person other than a citizen of the United States, who undertakes directly, by lease or other arrangement, to engage in air transportation.

Foreign air commerce means the carriage by aircraft of persons or property for compensation or hire, or the carriage of mail by aircraft, or the operation or navigation of aircraft in the conduct or furtherance of a business or vocation, in commerce between a place in the United States and any place outside thereof; whether such commerce moves wholly by aircraft or partly by aircraft and partly by other forms of transportation.

Foreign air transportation means the carriage by aircraft of persons or property as a common carrier for compensation or hire, or the carriage of mail by aircraft, in commerce between a place in the United States and any place outside of the United States, whether that commerce moves wholly by aircraft or partly by aircraft and partly by other forms of transportation.

Forward wing means a forward lifting surface of a canard configuration or tandem-wing configuration airplane. The surface may be a fixed, movable, or variable geometry surface, with or without control surfaces.

Full flight simulator (FFS) means a replica of a specific type; or make, model, and series aircraft cockpit. It includes the assemblage of equipment and computer programs necessary to represent aircraft operations in ground and flight conditions, a visual system providing an out-of-the-cockpit view, a system that provides cues at least equivalent to those of a three-degree-of-freedom motion system, and has the full range of capabilities of the systems installed in the device as described in part 60 of this chapter and the qualification performance standards (QPS) for a specific FFS qualification level.

Ground visibility means prevailing horizontal visibility near the earth's surface as reported by the United States National Weather Service or an accredited observer.

Go-around power or thrust setting means the maximum allowable in-flight power or thrust setting identified in the performance data.

Idle thrust means the jet thrust obtained with the engine power control level set at the stop for the least thrust position at which it can be placed.

IFR conditions means weather conditions below the minimum for flight under visual flight rules.

IFR over-the-top, with respect to the operation of aircraft, means the operation of an aircraft over-the-top on an IFR flight plan when cleared by air traffic control to maintain "VFR conditions" or "VFR conditions on top".

Indicated airspeed means the speed of an aircraft as shown on its pitot static airspeed indicator calibrated to reflect standard atmosphere adiabatic compressible flow at sea level uncorrected for airspeed system errors.

In-flight shutdown (IFSD) means, for ETOPS only, when an engine ceases to function (when the airplane is airborne) and is shutdown, whether self induced, flightcrew initiated or caused by an external influence. The FAA considers IFSD for all causes: for example, flameout, internal failure, flightcrew initiated shutdown, foreign object ingestion, icing, inability to obtain or control desired thrust or power, and cycling of the start control, however briefly, even if the engine operates normally for the remainder of the flight. This definition excludes the airborne cessation of the functioning of an engine when immediately followed by an automatic engine relight and when an engine does not achieve desired thrust or power but is not shutdown.

Instrument means a device using an internal mechanism to show visually or aurally the attitude, altitude, or operation of an aircraft or aircraft part. It includes electronic devices for automatically controlling an aircraft in flight.

Instrument approach procedure (IAP) is a series of predetermined maneuvers by reference to flight instruments with specified protection from obstacles and assurance of navigation signal reception capability. It begins from the initial approach fix, or where applicable, from the beginning of a defined arrival route to a point:

    1) From which a landing can be completed; or

    2) If a landing is not completed, to a position at which holding or en route obstacle clearance criteria apply.

Interstate air commerce means the carriage by aircraft of persons or property for compensation or hire, or the carriage of mail by aircraft, or the operation or navigation of aircraft in the conduct or furtherance of a business or vocation, in commerce between a place in any State of the

United States, or the District of Columbia, and a place in any other State of the United States, or the District of Columbia; or between places in the same State of the United States through the airspace over any place outside thereof; or between places in the same territory or possession of the United States, or the District of Columbia.

Interstate air transportation means the carriage by aircraft of persons or property as a common carrier for compensation or hire, or the carriage of mail by aircraft in commerce:

1) Between a place in a State or the District of Columbia and another place in another State or the District of Columbia;

2) Between places in the same State through the airspace over any place outside that State; or

3) Between places in the same possession of the United States;

Whether that commerce moves wholly by aircraft of partly by aircraft and partly by other forms of transportation.

Intrastate air transportation means the carriage of persons or property as a common carrier for compensation or hire, by turbojet-powered aircraft capable of carrying thirty or more persons, wholly within the same State of the United States.

Landing gear extended speed means the maximum speed at which an aircraft can be safely flown with the landing gear extended.

Landing gear operating speed means the maximum speed at which the landing gear can be safely extended or retracted.

Large aircraft means aircraft of more than 12,500 pounds, maximum certificated takeoff weight.

Load factor means the ratio of a specified load to the total weight of the aircraft. The specified load is expressed in terms of any of the following: aerodynamic forces, inertia forces, or ground or water reactions.

Long-range communication system (LRCS). A system that uses satellite relay, data link, high frequency, or another approved communication system which extends beyond line of sight.

Long-range navigation system (LRNS). An electronic navigation unit that is approved for use under instrument flight rules as a primary means of navigation, and has at least one source of navigational input, such as inertial navigation system or global positioning system.

Mach number means the ratio of true airspeed to the speed of sound.

Maintenance means inspection, overhaul, repair, preservation, and the replacement of parts, but excludes preventive maintenance.

Major alteration means an alteration not listed in the aircraft, aircraft engine, or propeller specifications–

  1) That might appreciably affect weight, balance, structural strength, performance, powerplant operation, flight characteristics, or other qualities affecting airworthiness; or

  2) That is not done according to accepted practices or cannot be done by elementary operations.

Major repair means a repair:

  1) That, if improperly done, might appreciably affect weight, balance, structural strength, performance, powerplant operation, flight characteristics, or other qualities affecting airworthiness; or

  2) That is not done according to accepted practices or cannot be done by elementary operations.

Manifold pressure means absolute pressure as measured at the appropriate point in the induction system and usually expressed in inches of mercury.

Maximum engine overtorque, as it applies to turbopropeller and turboshaft engines incorporating free power turbines for all ratings except one engine inoperative (OEI) ratings of two minutes or less, means the maximum torque of the free power turbine rotor assembly, the inadvertent occurrence of which, for periods of up to 20 seconds, will not require rejection of the engine from service, or any maintenance action other than to correct the cause.

Medical certificate means acceptable evidence of physical fitness on a form prescribed by the Administrator.

Military operations area. A military operations area (MOA) is airspace established outside Class A airspace to separate or segregate certain nonhazardous military activities from IFR Traffic and to identify for VFR traffic where theses activities are conducted.

Minimum descent altitude (MDA) is the lowest altitude specified in an instrument approach procedure, expressed in feet above mean sea level, to which descent is authorized on final approach or during circle-to-land maneuvering until the pilot sees the required visual references for the heliport or runway of intended landing.

Minor alteration means an alteration other than a major alteration.

Minor repair means a repair other than a major repair.

National defense airspace means airspace established by a regulation prescribed, or an order issued under, 49 U.S.C. 40103(b)(3).

Navigable airspace means airspace at and above the minimum flight altitudes prescribed by or under this chapter, including airspace needed for safe takeoff and landing.

Night means the time between the end of evening civil twilight and the beginning of morning civil twilight, as published in the Air Almanac, converted to local time.

Nonprecision approach procedure means a standard instrument approach procedure in which no electronic glide slope is provided.

Operate, with respect to aircraft, means use, cause to use or authorize to use aircraft, for the purpose (except as provided in § 91.13 of this chapter) of air navigation including the piloting of aircraft, with or without the right of legal control (as owner, lessee, or otherwise).

Operational control, with respect to a flight, means the exercise of authority over initiating, conducting or terminating a flight.

Overseas air commerce means the carriage by aircraft of persons or property for compensation or hire, or the carriage of mail by aircraft, or the operation or navigation of aircraft in the conduct or furtherance of a business or vocation, in commerce between a place in any State of the United States, or the District of Columbia, and any place in a territory or possession of the United States; or between a place in a territory or possession of the United States, and a place in any other territory or possession of the United States.

Overseas air transportation means the carriage by aircraft of persons or property as a common carrier for compensation or hire, or the carriage of mail by aircraft, in commerce:

1) Between a place in a State or the District of Columbia and a place in a possession of the United States; or

2) Between a place in a possession of the United States and a place in another possession of the United States; whether that commerce moves wholly by aircraft or partly by aircraft and partly by other forms of transportation.

Over-the-top means above the layer of clouds or other obscuring phenomena forming the ceiling.

Parachute means a device used or intended to be used to retard the fall of a body or object through the air.

Person means an individual, firm, partnership, corporation, company, association, joint-stock association, or governmental entity. It includes a trustee, receiver, assignee, or similar representative of any of them.

Pilotage means navigation by visual reference to landmarks.

Pilot in command means the person who:

1) Has final authority and responsibility for the operation and safety of the flight;

2) Has been designated as pilot in command before or during the flight; and

3) Holds the appropriate category, class, and type rating, if appropriate, for the conduct of the flight.

Pitch setting means the propeller blade setting as determined by the blade angle measured in a manner, and at a radius, specified by the instruction manual for the propeller.

Portable oxygen concentrator means a medical device that separates oxygen from other gasses in ambient air and dispenses this concentrated oxygen to the user.

Positive control means control of all air traffic, within designated airspace, by air traffic control.

Powered-lift means a heavier-than-air aircraft capable of vertical takeoff, vertical landing, and low speed flight that depends principally on engine-driven lift devices or engine thrust for lift during these flight regimes and on nonrotating airfoil(s) for lift during horizontal flight.

Precision approach procedure means a standard instrument approach procedure in which an electronic glide slope is provided, such as ILS and PAR.

Preventive maintenance means simple or minor preservation operations and the replacement of small standard parts not involving complex assembly operations.

Prohibited area. A prohibited area is airspace designated under part 73 within which no person may operate an aircraft without the permission of the using agency.

Propeller means a device for propelling an aircraft that has blades on an engine-driven shaft and that, when rotated, produces by its action on the air, a thrust approximately perpendicular to its plane of rotation. It includes control components normally supplied by its manufacturer, but does not include main and auxiliary rotors or rotating airfoils of engines.

Public aircraft means any of the following aircraft when not being used for a commercial purpose or to carry an individual other than a crewmember or qualified non-crewmember:

1) An aircraft used only for the United States Government; an aircraft owned by the Government and operated by any person for purposes related to crew training, equipment development, or demonstration;

an aircraft owned and operated by the government of a State, the District of Columbia, or a territory or possession of the United States or a political subdivision of one of these governments; or an aircraft exclusively leased for at least 90 continuous days by the government of a State, the District of Columbia, or a territory or possession of the United States or a political subdivision of one of these governments.

i) For the sole purpose of determining public aircraft status, **commercial purposes** means the transportation of persons or property for compensation or hire, but does not include the operation of an aircraft by the armed forces for reimbursement when that reimbursement is required by any Federal statute, regulation, or directive, in effect on November 1, 1999, or by one government on behalf of another government under a cost reimbursement agreement if the government on whose behalf the operation is conducted certifies to the Administrator of the Federal Aviation Administration that the operation is necessary to respond to a significant and imminent threat to life or property (including natural resources) and that no service by a private operator is reasonably available to meet the threat.

ii) For the sole purpose of determining public aircraft status, **governmental function** means an activity undertaken by a government, such as national defense, intelligence missions, firefighting, search and rescue, law enforcement (including transport of prisoners, detainees, and illegal aliens), aeronautical research, or biological or geological resource management.

iii) For the sole purpose of determining public aircraft status, **qualified non-crewmember** means an individual, other than a member of the crew, aboard an aircraft operated by the armed forces or an intelligence agency of the United States Government, or whose presence is required to perform, or is associated with the performance of, a governmental function.

2) *Armed forces aircraft.*

3) *National Guard Aircraft.*

Rated 30-second OEI Power, with respect to rotorcraft turbine engines, means the approved brake horsepower developed under static conditions at specified altitudes and temperatures within the operating limitations established for the engine under part 33 of this chapter, for continuation of one flight operation after the failure or shutdown of one engine in multiengine rotorcraft, for up to three periods of use no longer than 30 seconds each in any one flight, and followed by mandatory inspection and prescribed maintenance action.

Rated 2-minute OEI Power, with respect to rotorcraft turbine engines, means the approved brake horsepower developed under static conditions at specified altitudes and temperatures within the operating limitations established for the engine under part 33 of this chapter, for continuation of one flight operation after the failure or shutdown of one engine in multiengine rotorcraft, for up to three periods of use no longer than 2 minutes each in any one flight, and followed by mandatory inspection and prescribed maintenance action.

Rated continuous OEI power, with respect to rotorcraft turbine engines, means the approved brake horsepower developed under static conditions at specified altitudes and temperatures within the operating limitations established for the engine under part 33 of this chapter, and limited in use to the time required to complete the flight after the failure or shutdown of one engine of a multiengine rotorcraft.

Rated maximum continuous augmented thrust, with respect to turbojet engine type certification, means the approved jet thrust that is developed statically or in flight, in standard atmosphere at a specified altitude, with fluid injection or with the burning of fuel in a separate combustion chamber, within the engine operating limitations established under Part 33 of this chapter, and approved for unrestricted periods of use.

Rated maximum continuous power, with respect to reciprocating, turbopropeller, and turboshaft engines, means the approved brake horsepower that is developed statically or in flight, in standard atmosphere at a specified altitude, within the engine operating limitations established under part 33, and approved for unrestricted periods of use.

Rated maximum continuous thrust, with respect to turbojet engine type certification, means the approved jet thrust that is developed statically or in flight, in standard atmosphere at a specified altitude, without fluid injection and without the burning of fuel in a separate combustion chamber, within the engine operating limitations established under part 33 of this chapter, and approved for unrestricted periods of use.

Rated takeoff augmented thrust, with respect to turbojet engine type certification, means the approved jet thrust that is developed statically under standard sea level conditions, with fluid injection or with the burning of fuel in a separate combustion chamber, within the engine operating limitations established under part 33 of this chapter, and limited in use to periods of not over 5 minutes for takeoff operation.

Rated takeoff power, with respect to reciprocating, turbopropeller, and turboshaft engine type certification, means the approved brake horsepower that is developed statically under standard sea level conditions, within the engine operating limitations established under part 33, and limited in use to periods of not over 5 minutes for takeoff operation.

Rated takeoff thrust, with respect to turbojet engine type certification, means the approved jet thrust that is developed statically under standard sea level conditions, without fluid injection and without the burning of fuel in a separate combustion chamber, within the engine operating limitations established under part 33 of this chapter, and limited in use to periods of not over 5 minutes for takeoff operation.

Rated 30-minute OEI power, with respect to rotorcraft turbine engines, means the approved brake horsepower developed under static conditions at specified altitudes and temperatures within the operating limitations established for the engine under part 33 of this chapter, and limited in use to one period of use no longer than 30 minutes after the failure or shutdown of one engine of a multiengine rotorcraft.

Rated 2½-minute OEI power, with respect to rotorcraft turbine engines, means the approved brake horsepower developed under static conditions at specified altitudes and temperatures within the operating limitations established for the engine under part 33 of this chapter for periods of use no longer than 21/2 minutes each after the failure or shutdown of one engine of a multiengine rotorcraft.

Rating means a statement that, as a part of a certificate, sets forth special conditions, privileges, or limitations.

Reference landing speed means the speed of the airplane, in a specified landing configuration, at the point where it descends through the 50 foot height in the determination of the landing distance.

Reporting point means a geographical location in relation to which the position of an aircraft is reported.

Restricted area. A restricted area is airspace designated under Part 73 within which the flight of aircraft, while not wholly prohibited, is subject to restriction.

Route segment is a portion of a route bounded on each end by a fix or navigation aid (NAVAID).

Sea level engine means a reciprocating aircraft engine having a rated takeoff power that is producible only at sea level.

Second in command means a pilot who is designated to be second in command of an aircraft during flight time.

Show, unless the context otherwise requires, means to show to the satisfaction of the Administrator.

Small aircraft means aircraft of 12,500 pounds or less, maximum certificated takeoff weight.

Special VFR conditions mean meteorological conditions that are less than those required for basic VFR flight in controlled airspace and in which some aircraft are permitted flight under visual flight rules.

Special VFR operations means aircraft operating in accordance with clearances within controlled airspace in meteorological conditions less than the basic VFR weather minima. Such operations must be requested by the pilot and approved by ATC.

Standard atmosphere means the atmosphere defined in U.S. Standard Atmosphere, 1962 (Geopotential altitude tables).

Stopway means an area beyond the takeoff runway, no less wide than the runway and centered upon the extended centerline of the runway, able to support the airplane during an aborted takeoff, without causing structural damage to the airplane, and designated by the airport authorities for use in decelerating the airplane during an aborted takeoff.

Suitable RNAV system is an RNAV system that meets the required performance established for a type of operation, e.g. IFR; and is suitable for operation over the route to be flown in terms of any performance criteria (including accuracy) established by the air navigation service provider for certain routes (e.g. oceanic, ATS routes, and IAPs). An RNAV system's suitability is dependent upon the availability of ground and/or satellite navigation aids that are needed to meet any route performance criteria that may be prescribed in route specifications to navigate the aircraft along the route to be flown. Information on suitable RNAV systems is published in FAA guidance material.

Synthetic vision means a computer-generated image of the external scene topography from the perspective of the flight deck that is derived from aircraft attitude, high-precision navigation solution, and database of terrain, obstacles and relevant cultural features.

Synthetic vision system means an electronic means to display a synthetic vision image of the external scene topography to the flight crew.

Takeoff power:

1) With respect to reciprocating engines, means the brake horsepower that is developed under standard sea level conditions, and under the maximum conditions of crankshaft rotational speed and engine manifold pressure approved for the normal takeoff, and limited in continuous use to the period of time shown in the approved engine specification; and

2) With respect to turbine engines, means the brake horsepower that is developed under static conditions at a specified altitude and atmospheric temperature, and under the maximum conditions of rotor shaft

rotational speed and gas temperature approved for the normal take-off, and limited in continuous use to the period of time shown in the approved engine specification.

Takeoff safety speed means a referenced airspeed obtained after lift-off at which the required one-engine-inoperative climb performance can be achieved.

Takeoff thrust, with respect to turbine engines, means the jet thrust that is developed under static conditions at a specific altitude and atmospheric temperature under the maximum conditions of rotorshaft rotational speed and gas temperature approved for the normal takeoff, and limited in continuous use to the period of time shown in the approved engine specification.

Tandem wing configuration means a configuration having two wings of similar span, mounted in tandem.

TCAS I means a TCAS that utilizes interrogations of, and replies from, airborne radar beacon transponders and provides traffic advisories to the pilot.

TCAS II means a TCAS that utilizes interrogations of, and replies from airborne radar beacon transponders and provides traffic advisories and resolution advisories in the vertical plane.

TCAS III means a TCAS that utilizes interrogation of, and replies from, airborne radar beacon transponders and provides traffic advisories and resolution advisories in the vertical and horizontal planes to the pilot.

Time in service, with respect to maintenance time records, means the time from the moment an aircraft leaves the surface of the earth until it touches it at the next point of landing.

Traffic pattern means the traffic flow that is prescribed for aircraft landing at, taxiing on, or taking off from, an airport.

True airspeed means the airspeed of an aircraft relative to undisturbed air. True airspeed is equal to equivalent airspeed multiplied by $(\rho 0/\rho)1/2$.

Type:

1) As used with respect to the certification, ratings, privileges, and limitations of airmen, means a specific make and basic model of aircraft, including modifications thereto that do not change its handling or flight characteristics. Examples include: DC-7, 1049, and F-27; and

2) As used with respect to the certification of aircraft, means those aircraft which are similar in design. Examples include: DC-7 and DC-7C; 1049G and 1049H; and F-27 and F-27F.

3) As used with respect to the certification of aircraft engines means those engines which are similar in design. For example, JT8D and JT8D-7 are engines of the same type, and JT9D-3A and JT9D-7 are engines of the same type.

United States, in a geographical sense, means (1) the States, the District of Columbia, Puerto Rico, and the possessions, including the territorial waters, and (2) the airspace of those areas.

United States air carrier means a citizen of the United States who undertakes directly by lease, or other arrangement, to engage in air transportation.

VFR over-the-top, with respect to the operation of aircraft, means the operation of an aircraft over-the-top under VFR when it is not being operated on an IFR flight plan.

Warning area. A warning area is airspace of defined dimensions, extending from 3 nautical miles outward from the coast of the United States, that contains activity that may be hazardous to nonparticipating aircraft. The purpose of such warning areas is to warn nonparticipating pilots of the potential danger. A warning area may be located over domestic or international waters or both.

Winglet or tip fin means an out-of-plane surface extending from a lifting surface. The surface may or may not have control surfaces.

§ 1.2 Abbreviations and symbols.

In Subchapters A through K of this chapter:

AFM means airplane flight manual.

AGL means above ground level.

ALS means approach light system.

APU means auxiliary power unit.

ASR means airport surveillance radar.

ATC means air traffic control.

ATS means Air Traffic Service.

CAS means calibrated airspeed.

CAT II means Category II.

DH means decision height.

DME means distance measuring equipment compatible with TACAN.

EAS means equivalent airspeed.

EFVS means enhanced flight vision system.

Equi-Time Point means a point on the route of flight where the flight time, considering wind, to each of two selected airports is equal.

ETOPS means extended operations.

FAA means Federal Aviation Administration.

FFS means full flight simulator.

FM means fan marker.

FSTD means flight simulation training device.

FTD means flight training device.

GS means glide slope.

HIRL means high-intensity runway light system.

IAS means indicated airspeed.

ICAO means International Civil Aviation Organization.

IFR means instrument flight rules.

IFSD means in-flight shutdown.

ILS means instrument landing system.

IM means ILS inner marker.

INT means intersection.

LDA means localizer-type directional aid.

LFR means low-frequency radio range.

LMM means compass locator at middle marker.

LOC means ILS localizer.

LOM means compass locator at outer marker.

M means mach number.

MAA means maximum authorized IFR altitude.

MALS means medium intensity approach light system.

MALSR means medium intensity approach light system with runway alignment indicator lights.

MCA means minimum crossing altitude.

MDA means minimum descent altitude.

MEA means minimum en route IFR altitude.

MEL means minimum equipment list.

MM means ILS middle marker.

MOCA means minimum obstruction clearance altitude.

MRA means minimum reception altitude.

MSL means mean sea level.

NDB (ADF) means nondirectional beacon (automatic direction finder).

NM means nautical mile.

NOPAC means North Pacific area of operation.

NOPT means no procedure turn required.

OEI means one engine inoperative.

OM means ILS outer marker.

OPSPECS means operations specifications.

PACOTS means Pacific Organized Track System.

PAR means precision approach radar.

PMA means parts manufacturer approval.

POC means portable oxygen concentrator.

PTRS means Performance Tracking and Reporting System.

RAIL means runway alignment indicator light system.

RBN means radio beacon.

RCLM means runway centerline marking.

RCLS means runway centerline light system.

REIL means runway end identification lights.

RFFS means rescue and firefighting services.

RNAV means area navigation.

RR means low or medium frequency radio range station.

RVR means runway visual range as measured in the touchdown zone area.

SALS means short approach light system.

SATCOM means satellite communications.

SSALS means simplified short approach light system.

SSALSR means simplified short approach light system with runway alignment indicator lights.

TACAN means ultra-high frequency tactical air navigational aid.

TAS means true airspeed.

TCAS means a traffic alert and collision avoidance system.

TDZL means touchdown zone lights.

TSO means technical standard order.

TVOR means very high frequency terminal omnirange station.

V_A means design maneuvering speed.

V_B means design speed for maximum gust intensity.

V_C means design cruising speed.

V_D means design diving speed.

V_{DF}/M_{DF} means demonstrated flight diving speed.

V_{EF} means the speed at which the critical engine is assumed to fail during takeoff.

V_F means design flap speed.

V_{FC}/M_{FC} means maximum speed for stability characteristics.

V_{FE} means maximum flap extended speed.

V_{FTO} means final takeoff speed.

V_H means maximum speed in level flight with maximum continuous power.

V_{LE} means maximum landing gear extended speed.

V_{LO} means maximum landing gear operating speed.

V_{LOF} means lift-off speed.

V_{MC} means minimum control speed with the critical engine inoperative.

V_{MO}/M_{MO} means maximum operating limit speed.

V_{MU} means minimum unstick speed.

V_{NE} means never-exceed speed.

V$_{NO}$ means maximum structural cruising speed.

V$_R$ means rotation speed.

V$_{REF}$ means reference landing speed.

V$_S$ means the stalling speed or the minimum steady flight speed at which the airplane is controllable.

V$_{S0}$ means the stalling speed or the minimum steady flight speed in the landing configuration.

V$_{S1}$ means the stalling speed or the minimum steady flight speed obtained in a specific configuration.

V$_{SR}$ means reference stall speed.

V$_{SR0}$ means reference stall speed in the landing configuration.

V$_{SR1}$ means reference stall speed in a specific configuration.

V$_{SW}$ means speed at which onset of natural or artificial stall warning occurs.

V$_{TOSS}$ means takeoff safety speed for Category A rotorcraft.

V$_X$ means speed for best angle of climb.

V$_Y$ means speed for best rate of climb.

V$_1$ means the maximum speed in the takeoff at which the pilot must take the first action (e.g., apply brakes, reduce thrust, deploy speed brakes) to stop the airplane within the accelerate-stop distance. V$_1$ also means the minimum speed in the takeoff, following a failure of the critical engine at V$_{EF}$, at which the pilot can continue the takeoff and achieve the required height above the takeoff surface within the takeoff distance.

V$_2$ means takeoff safety speed.

V$_{2min}$ means minimum takeoff safety speed.

VFR means visual flight rules.

VGSI means visual glide slope indicator.

VHF means very high frequency.

VOR means very high frequency omnirange station.

VORTAC means collocated VOR and TACAN.

§ 1.3 Rules of construction.

a) In Subchapters A through K of this chapter, unless the context requires otherwise:

1) Words importing the singular include the plural;

2) Words importing the plural include the singular; and

3) Words importing the masculine gender include the feminine.

b) In Subchapters A through K of this chapter, the word:

1) **Shall** is used in an imperative sense;

2) **May** is used in a permissive sense to state authority or permission to do the act prescribed, and the words "no person may * * *" or "a person may not * * *" mean that no person is required, authorized, or permitted to do the act prescribed; and

3) **Includes** means "includes but is not limited to".

Title 14 CFR, Part 23

Airworthiness Standards: Normal Category Airplanes

§ 23.2005 Certification of normal category airplanes.

a) Certification in the normal category applies to airplanes with a passenger-seating configuration of 19 or less and a maximum certificated take-off weight of 19,000 pounds or less.

b) Airplane certification levels are:

1) Level 1–for airplanes with a maximum seating configuration of 0 to 1 passengers.

2) Level 2–for airplanes with a maximum seating configuration of 2 to 6 passengers.

3) Level 3–for airplanes with a maximum seating configuration of 7 to 9 passengers.

4) Level 4–for airplanes with a maximum seating configuration of 10 to 19 passengers.

c) Airplane performance levels are:

1) Low speed–for airplanes with a VNO and VMO ≤ 250 Knots Calibrated Airspeed (KCAS) and a MMO ≤ 0.6.

2) High speed–for airplanes with a VNO or VMO > 250 KCAS or a MMO > 0.6.

d) Airplanes not certified for aerobatics may be used to perform any maneuver incident to normal flying, including–

1) Stalls (except whip stalls); and

2) Lazy eights, chandelles, and steep turns, in which the angle of bank is not more than 60 degrees.

e) Airplanes certified for aerobatics may be used to perform maneuvers without limitations, other than those limitations established under subpart G of this part.

Title 14 CFR, Part 43

Maintenance, Preventive Maintenance, Rebuilding, and Alteration

Appendix A to Part 43

Major Alterations, Major Repairs, and Preventive Maintenance

a) **Major alterations–**

1) **Airframe major alterations**. Alterations of the following parts and alterations of the following types, when not listed in the aircraft specifications issued by the FAA, are airframe major alterations:

i) Wings.

ii) Tail surfaces.

iii) Fuselage.

iv) Engine mounts.

v) Control system.

vi) Landing gear.

vii) Hull or floats.

viii) Elements of an airframe including spars, ribs, fittings, shock absorbers, bracing, cowling, fairings, and balance weights.

ix) Hydraulic and electrical actuating system of components.

x) Rotor blades.

xi) Changes to the empty weight or empty balance which result in an increase in the maximum certificated weight or center of gravity limits of the aircraft.

xii) Changes to the basic design of the fuel, oil, cooling, heating, cabin pressurization, electrical, hydraulic, de-icing, or exhaust systems.

xiii) Changes to the wing or to fixed or movable control surfaces which affect flutter and vibration characteristics.

2) **Powerplant major alterations**. The following alterations of a powerplant when not listed in the engine specifications issued by the FAA, are powerplant major alterations.

i) Conversion of an aircraft engine from one approved model to another, involving any changes in compression ratio, propeller reduction gear, impeller gear ratios or the substitution of major engine parts which requires extensive rework and testing of the engine.

ii) Changes to the engine by replacing aircraft engine structural parts with parts not supplied by the original manufacturer or parts not specifically approved by the Administrator.

iii) Installation of an accessory which is not approved for the engine.

iv) Removal of accessories that are listed as required equipment on the aircraft or engine specification.

v) Installation of structural parts other than the type of parts approved for the installation.

vi) Conversions of any sort for the purpose of using fuel of a rating or grade other than that listed in the engine specifications.

3) **Propeller major alterations**. The following alterations of a propeller when not authorized in the propeller specifications issued by the FAA are propeller major alterations:

i) Changes in blade design.

ii) Changes in hub design.

iii) Changes in the governor or control design.

iv) Installation of a propeller governor or feathering system.

v) Installation of propeller de-icing system.

vi) Installation of parts not approved for the propeller.

4) **Appliance major alterations**. Alterations of the basic design not made in accordance with recommendations of the appliance manufacturer or in accordance with an FAA Airworthiness Directive are

appliance major alterations. In addition, changes in the basic design of radio communication and navigation equipment approved under type certification or a Technical Standard Order that have an effect on frequency stability, noise level, sensitivity, selectivity, distortion, spurious radiation, AVC characteristics, or ability to meet environmental test conditions and other changes that have an effect on the performance of the equipment are also major alterations.

b) **Major repairs**–

1) **Airframe major repairs**. Repairs to the following parts of an airframe and repairs of the following types, involving the strengthening, reinforcing, splicing, and manufacturing of primary structural members or their replacement, when replacement is by fabrication such as riveting or welding, are airframe major repairs.

i) Box beams.

ii) Monocoque or semimonocoque wings or control surfaces.

iii) Wing stringers or chord members.

iv) Spars.

v) Spar flanges.

vi) Members of truss-type beams.

vii) Thin sheet webs of beams.

viii) Keel and chine members of boat hulls or floats.

ix) Corrugated sheet compression members which act as flange material of wings or tail surfaces.

x) Wing main ribs and compression members.

xi) Wing or tail surface brace struts.

xii) Engine mounts.

xiii) Fuselage longerons.

xiv) Members of the side truss, horizontal truss, or bulkheads.

xv) Main seat support braces and brackets.

xvi) Landing gear brace struts.

xvii) Axles.

xviii) Wheels.

xix) Skis, and ski pedestals.

xx) Parts of the control system such as control columns, pedals, shafts, brackets, or horns.

xxi) Repairs involving the substitution of material.

xxii) The repair of damaged areas in metal or plywood stressed covering exceeding six inches in any direction.

xxiii) The repair of portions of skin sheets by making additional seams.

xxiv) The splicing of skin sheets.

xxv) The repair of three or more adjacent wing or control surface ribs or the leading edge of wings and control surfaces, between such adjacent ribs.

xxvi) Repair of fabric covering involving an area greater than that required to repair two adjacent ribs.

xxvii) Replacement of fabric on fabric covered parts such as wings, fuselages, stabilizers, and control surfaces.

xxviii) Repairing, including rebottoming, of removable or integral fuel tanks and oil tanks.

2) **Powerplant major repairs**. Repairs of the following parts of an engine and repairs of the following types, are powerplant major repairs:

i) Separation or disassembly of a crankcase or crankshaft of a reciprocating engine equipped with an integral supercharger.

ii) Separation or disassembly of a crankcase or crankshaft of a reciprocating engine equipped with other than spur-type propeller reduction gearing.

iii) Special repairs to structural engine parts by welding, plating, metalizing, or other methods.

3) **Propeller major repairs**. Repairs of the following types to a propeller are propeller major repairs:

i) Any repairs to, or straightening of steel blades.

ii) Repairing or machining of steel hubs.

iii) Shortening of blades.

iv) Retipping of wood propellers.

v) Replacement of outer laminations on fixed pitch wood propellers.

vi) Repairing elongated bolt holes in the hub of fixed pitch wood propellers.

vii) Inlay work on wood blades.

viii) Repairs to composition blades.

ix) Replacement of tip fabric.

x) Replacement of plastic covering.

xi) Repair of propeller governors.

xii) Overhaul of controllable pitch propellers.

xiii) Repairs to deep dents, cuts, scars, nicks, etc., and straightening of aluminum blades.

xiv) The repair or replacement of internal elements of blades.

4) **Appliance major repairs**. Repairs of the following types to appliances are appliance major repairs:

i) Calibration and repair of instruments.

ii) Calibration of radio equipment.

iii) Rewinding the field coil of an electrical accessory.

iv) Complete disassembly of complex hydraulic power valves.

v) Overhaul of pressure type carburetors, and pressure type fuel, oil and hydraulic pumps.

c) **Preventive maintenance**. Preventive maintenance is limited to the following work, provided it does not involve complex assembly operations:

1) Removal, installation, and repair of landing gear tires.

2) Replacing elastic shock absorber cords on landing gear.

3) Servicing landing gear shock struts by adding oil, air, or both.

4) Servicing landing gear wheel bearings, such as cleaning and greasing.

5) Replacing defective safety wiring or cotter keys.

6) Lubrication not requiring disassembly other than removal of non-structural items such as cover plates, cowlings, and fairings.

7) Making simple fabric patches not requiring rib stitching or the removal of structural parts or control surfaces. In the case of balloons, the making of small fabric repairs to envelopes (as defined in, and in accordance with, the balloon manufacturers' instructions) not requiring load tape repair or replacement.

8) Replenishing hydraulic fluid in the hydraulic reservoir.

9) Refinishing decorative coating of fuselage, balloon baskets, wings tail group surfaces (excluding balanced control surfaces), fairings, cowlings, landing gear, cabin, or cockpit interior when removal or disassembly of any primary structure or operating system is not required.

10) Applying preservative or protective material to components where no disassembly of any primary structure or operating system is involved and where such coating is not prohibited or is not contrary to good practices.

11) Repairing upholstery and decorative furnishings of the cabin, cockpit, or balloon basket interior when the repairing does not require disassembly of any primary structure or operating system or interfere with an operating system or affect the primary structure of the aircraft.

12) Making small simple repairs to fairings, nonstructural cover plates, cowlings, and small patches and reinforcements not changing the contour so as to interfere with proper air flow.

13) Replacing side windows where that work does not interfere with the structure or any operating system such as controls, electrical equipment, etc.

14) Replacing safety belts.

15) Replacing seats or seat parts with replacement parts approved for the aircraft, not involving disassembly of any primary structure or operating system.

16) Trouble shooting and repairing broken circuits in landing light wiring circuits.

17) Replacing bulbs, reflectors, and lenses of position and landing lights.

18) Replacing wheels and skis where no weight and balance computation is involved.

19) Replacing any cowling not requiring removal of the propeller or disconnection of flight controls.

20) Replacing or cleaning spark plugs and setting of spark plug gap clearance.

21) Replacing any hose connection except hydraulic connections.

22) Replacing prefabricated fuel lines.

23) Cleaning or replacing fuel and oil strainers or filter elements.

24) Replacing and servicing batteries.

25) Cleaning of balloon burner pilot and main nozzles in accordance with the balloon manufacturer's instructions.

26) Replacement or adjustment of nonstructural standard fasteners incidental to operations.

27) The interchange of balloon baskets and burners on envelopes when the basket or burner is designated as interchangeable in the balloon type certificate data and the baskets and burners are specifically designed for quick removal and installation.

28) The installations of anti-misfueling devices to reduce the diameter of fuel tank filler openings provided the specific device has been made a part of the aircraft type certificate data by the aircraft manufacturer, the aircraft manufacturer has provided FAA-approved instructions for installation of the specific device, and installation does not involve the disassembly of the existing tank filler opening.

29) Removing, checking, and replacing magnetic chip detectors.

30) The inspection and maintenance tasks prescribed and specifically identified as preventive maintenance in a primary category aircraft type certificate or supplemental type certificate holder's approved special inspection and preventive maintenance program when accomplished on a primary category aircraft provided:

i) They are performed by the holder of at least a private pilot certificate issued under part 61 who is the registered owner (including co-owners) of the affected aircraft and who holds a certificate of competency for the affected aircraft (1) issued by a school approved under § 147.21(e) of this chapter; (2) issued by the holder of the production certificate for that primary category aircraft that has a special training program approved under § 21.24 of this subchapter; or (3) issued by another entity that has a course approved by the Administrator; and

ii) The inspections and maintenance tasks are performed in accordance with instructions contained by the special inspection and preventive maintenance program approved as part of the aircraft's type design or supplemental type design.

31) Removing and replacing self-contained, front instrument panel-mounted navigation and communication devices that employ tray-mounted connectors that connect the unit when the unit is installed into the instrument panel, (excluding automatic flight control systems, transponders, and microwave frequency distance measuring equipment (DME)). The approved unit must be designed to be readily and repeatedly removed and replaced, and pertinent instructions must be provided. Prior to the unit's intended use, and operational check must be performed in accordance with the applicable sections of part 91 of this chapter.

Appendix D to Part 43

Scope and Detail of Items (as Applicable to the Particular Aircraft) To Be Included in Annual and 100-Hour Inspections

a) Each person performing an annual or 100-hour inspection shall, before that inspection, remove or open all necessary inspection plates, access doors, fairing, and cowling. He shall thoroughly clean the aircraft and aircraft engine.

b) Each person performing an annual or 100-hour inspection shall inspect (where applicable) the following components of the fuselage and hull group:

1) Fabric and skin–for deterioration, distortion, other evidence of failure, and defective or insecure attachment of fittings.

2) Systems and components–for improper installation, apparent defects, and unsatisfactory operation.

3) Envelope, gas bags, ballast tanks, and related parts–for poor condition.

c) Each person performing an annual or 100-hour inspection shall inspect (where applicable) the following components of the cabin and cockpit group:

1) Generally–for uncleanliness and loose equipment that might foul the controls.

2) Seats and safety belts–for poor condition and apparent defects.

3) Windows and windshields–for deterioration and breakage.

4) Instruments–for poor condition, mounting, marking, and (where practicable) improper operation.

5) Flight and engine controls–for improper installation and improper operation.

6) Batteries–for improper installation and improper charge.

7) All systems–for improper installation, poor general condition, apparent and obvious defects, and insecurity of attachment.

d) Each person performing an annual or 100-hour inspection shall inspect (where applicable) components of the engine and nacelle group as follows:

1) Engine section–for visual evidence of excessive oil, fuel, or hydraulic leaks, and sources of such leaks.

2) Studs and nuts–for improper torquing and obvious defects.

3) Internal engine–for cylinder compression and for metal particles or foreign matter on screens and sump drain plugs. If there is weak cylinder compression, for improper internal condition and improper internal tolerances.

4) Engine mount–for cracks, looseness of mounting, and looseness of engine to mount.

5) Flexible vibration dampeners–for poor condition and deterioration.

6) Engine controls–for defects, improper travel, and improper safetying.

7) Lines, hoses, and clamps–for leaks, improper condition and looseness.

8) Exhaust stacks–for cracks, defects, and improper attachment.

9) Accessories–for apparent defects in security of mounting.

10) All systems–for improper installation, poor general condition, defects, and insecure attachment.

11) Cowling–for cracks, and defects.

e) Each person performing an annual or 100-hour inspection shall inspect (where applicable) the following components of the landing gear group:

1) All units–for poor condition and insecurity of attachment.

2) Shock absorbing devices–for improper oleo fluid level.

3) Linkages, trusses, and members–for undue or excessive wear fatigue, and distortion.

4) Retracting and locking mechanism–for improper operation.

5) Hydraulic lines–for leakage.

6) Electrical system–for chafing and improper operation of switches.

7) Wheels–for cracks, defects, and condition of bearings.

8) Tires–for wear and cuts.

9) Brakes–for improper adjustment.

10) Floats and skis–for insecure attachment and obvious or apparent defects.

f) Each person performing an annual or 100-hour inspection shall inspect (where applicable) all components of the wing and center section assembly for poor general condition, fabric or skin deterioration, distortion, evidence of failure, and insecurity of attachment.

g) Each person performing an annual or 100-hour inspection shall inspect (where applicable) all components and systems that make up the complete empennage assembly for poor general condition, fabric or skin deterioration, distortion, evidence of failure, insecure attachment, improper component installation, and improper component operation.

h) Each person performing an annual or 100-hour inspection shall inspect (where applicable) the following components of the propeller group:

1) Propeller assembly–for cracks, nicks, binds, and oil leakage.

2) Bolts–for improper torquing and lack of safetying.

3) Anti-icing devices–for improper operations and obvious defects.

4) Control mechanisms–for improper operation, insecure mounting, and restricted travel.

i) Each person performing an annual or 100-hour inspection shall inspect (where applicable) the following components of the radio group:

1) Radio and electronic equipment–for improper installation and insecure mounting.

2) Wiring and conduits–for improper routing, insecure mounting, and obvious defects.

3) Bonding and shielding–for improper installation and poor condition.

4) Antenna including trailing antenna–for poor condition, insecure mounting, and improper operation.

j) Each person performing an annual or 100-hour inspection shall inspect (where applicable) each installed miscellaneous item that is not otherwise covered by this listing for improper installation and improper operation.

Title 14 CFR, Part 61

Certification: Pilots, Flight Instructors, and Ground Instructors

§ 61.1 Applicability and definitions.

a) Except as provided in part 107 of this chapter, this part prescribes:

1) The requirements for issuing pilot, flight instructor, and ground instructor certificates and ratings; the conditions under which those certificates and ratings are necessary; and the privileges and limitations of those certificates and ratings.

2) The requirements for issuing pilot, flight instructor, and ground instructor authorizations; the conditions under which those authorizations are necessary; and the privileges and limitations of those authorizations.

3) The requirements for issuing pilot, flight instructor, and ground instructor certificates and ratings for persons who have taken courses approved by the Administrator under other parts of this chapter.

b) For the purpose of this part:

Aeronautical experience means pilot time obtained in an aircraft, flight simulator, or flight training device for meeting the appropriate training and flight time requirements for an airman certificate, rating, flight review, or recency of flight experience requirements of this part.

Authorized instructor means–

i) A person who holds a ground instructor certificate issued under part 61 of this chapter and is in compliance with § 61.217, when conducting ground training in accordance with the privileges and limitations of his or her ground instructor certificate;

ii) A person who holds a flight instructor certificate issued under part 61 of this chapter and is in compliance with § 61.197, when conducting ground training or flight training in accordance with the privileges and limitations of his or her flight instructor certificate; or

iii) A person authorized by the Administrator to provide ground training or flight training under part 61, 121, 135, or 142 of this chapter when conducting ground training or flight training in accordance with that authority.

Aviation training device means a training device, other than a full flight simulator or flight training device, that has been evaluated, qualified, and approved by the Administrator.

Complex airplane means an airplane that has a retractable landing gear, flaps, and a controllable pitch propeller, including airplanes equipped with an engine control system consisting of a digital computer and associated accessories for controlling the engine and propeller, such as a full authority digital engine control; or, in the case of a seaplane, flaps and a controllable pitch propeller, including seaplanes equipped with an engine control system consisting of a digital computer and associated accessories for controlling the engine and propeller, such as a full authority digital engine control.

Cross-country time means–

i) Except as provided in paragraphs (ii) through (vi) of this definition, time acquired during flight–

(A) Conducted by a person who holds a pilot certificate;

(B) Conducted in an aircraft;

(C) That includes a landing at a point other than the point of departure; and

(D) That involves the use of dead reckoning, pilotage, electronic navigation aids, radio aids, or other navigation systems to navigate to the landing point.

ii) For the purpose of meeting the aeronautical experience requirements (except for a rotorcraft category rating), for a private pilot certificate (except for a powered parachute category rating), a commercial pilot certificate, or an instrument rating, or for the purpose of exercising recreational pilot privileges (except in a rotorcraft) under § 61.101 (c), time acquired during a flight–

(A) Conducted in an appropriate aircraft;

(B) That includes a point of landing that was at least a straight-line distance of more than 50 nautical miles from the original point of departure; and

(C) That involves the use of dead reckoning, pilotage, electronic navigation aids, radio aids, or other navigation systems to navigate to the landing point.

iii) *Sport pilot certificates.*

iv) *Powered parachute certificates.*

v) *Rotorcraft certificates.*

vi) *Certain airline transport pilot certificates.*

vii) For a military pilot who qualifies for a commercial pilot certificate (except with a rotorcraft category rating) under § 61.73 of this part, time acquired during a flight–

(A) Conducted in an appropriate aircraft;

(B) That is at least a straight-line distance of more than 50 nautical miles from the original point of departure; and

(C) That involves the use of dead reckoning, pilotage, electronic navigation aids, radio aids, or other navigation systems.

Examiner means any person who is authorized by the Administrator to conduct a pilot proficiency test or a practical test for an airman certificate or rating issued under this part, or a person who is authorized to conduct a knowledge test under this part.

Flight training means that training, other than ground training, received from an authorized instructor in flight in an aircraft.

Ground training means that training, other than flight training, received from an authorized instructor.

Instrument approach means an approach procedure defined in part 97 of this chapter.

Instrument training means that time in which instrument training is received from an authorized instructor under actual or simulated instrument conditions.

Knowledge test means a test on the aeronautical knowledge areas required for an airman certificate or rating that can be administered in written form or by a computer.

Pilot time means that time in which a person–

i) Serves as a required pilot flight crewmember;

ii) Receives training from an authorized instructor in an aircraft, full flight simulator, flight training device, or aviation training device;

iii) Gives training as an authorized instructor in an aircraft, full flight simulator, flight training device, or aviation training device; or

iv) Serves as second in command in operations conducted in accordance with § 135.99(c) of this chapter when a second pilot is not required under the type certification of the aircraft or the regulations under which the flight is being conducted, provided the requirements in § 61.159(c) are satisfied.

Practical test means a test on the areas of operations for an airman certificate, rating, or authorization that is conducted by having the applicant respond to questions and demonstrate maneuvers in flight, in a flight simulator, or in a flight training device.

Set of aircraft means aircraft that share similar performance characteristics, such as similar airspeed and altitude operating envelopes, similar handling characteristics, and the same number and type of propulsion systems.

i) To exercise student pilot privileges from a certificated flight instructor with a sport pilot rating; or

ii) That includes a limitation for the operation of a light-sport aircraft specified in § 61.89(c) issued by a certificated flight instructor with other than a sport pilot rating.

Technically advanced airplane (TAA) means an airplane equipped with an electronically advanced avionics system.

Training time means training received–

> i) In flight from an authorized instructor;

> ii) On the ground from an authorized instructor; or

> iii) In a flight simulator or flight training device from an authorized instructor.

§ 61.3 Requirement for certificates, ratings, and authorizations.

a) **Required pilot certificate for operating a civil aircraft of the United States**. No person may serve as a required pilot flight crewmember of a civil aircraft of the United States, unless that person:

> 1) Has in the person's physical possession or readily accessible in the aircraft when exercising the privileges of that pilot certificate or authorization–

> i) A pilot certificate issued under this part and in accordance with § 61.19;

> ii) *A special purpose pilot authorization*;

> iii) *A temporary certificate*;

> iv) *A document conveying temporary authority*;

> v) *Part 119 certificate holders*;

> vi) *Fractional operations*; or

> vii) *Foreign operations*.

> 2) Has a photo identification that is in that person's physical possession or readily accessible in the aircraft when exercising the privileges of that pilot certificate or authorization. The photo identification must be a:

i) Driver's license issued by a State, the District of Columbia, or territory or possession of the United States;

ii) *Government identification card*;

iii) *U.S. Armed Forces' identification card*;

iv) Official passport;

v) *49 CFR part 1542 credentials*; or

vi) Other form of identification that the Administrator finds acceptable.

b) **Required pilot certificate for operating a foreign-registered aircraft within the United States**. No person may serve as a required pilot flight crewmember of a civil aircraft of foreign registry within the United States, unless–

1) That person's pilot certificate or document issued under § 61.29(e) is in that person's physical possession or readily accessible in the aircraft when exercising the privileges of that pilot certificate; and

2) Has been issued in accordance with this part, or has been issued or validated by the country in which the aircraft is registered.

c) **Medical certificate**.

1) A person may serve as a required pilot flight crewmember of an aircraft only if that person holds the appropriate medical certificate issued under part 67 of this chapter, or other documentation acceptable to the FAA, that is in that person's physical possession or readily accessible in the aircraft. Paragraph (c)(2) of this section provides certain exceptions to the requirement to hold a medical certificate.

2) A person is not required to meet the requirements of paragraph (c)(1) of this section if that person–

i) *Student pilots in gliders and balloons*;

ii) *Certain sport pilot operations*;

iii) *Student pilots in weight shift control*;

iv) *Certain sport pilot operations in glider or balloon privileges;*

v) *Certain sport pilot operations in glider or balloon privileges.*

vi) *Certain balloon operations;*

vii) *Certain glider operations;*

viii) *Certain flight instructor operations;*

ix) *Ground instructor operations;*

x) *Foreign country operations;*

xi) Is operating an aircraft with a U.S. pilot certificate, issued on the basis of a foreign pilot license, issued under § 61.75, and holds a medical certificate issued by the foreign country that issued the foreign pilot license, which is in that person's physical possession or readily accessible in the aircraft when exercising the privileges of that airman certificate;

xii) *Military pilots;*

xiii) *Certain student, recreational or private pilot certificate operations;* or

xiv) *Certain flight instructor operations.*

d) *Flight instructor certificate.*

e) *Instrument rating.*

f) *Category II pilot authorization.*

g) *Category III pilot authorization.*

h) *Category A aircraft pilot authorization.*

i) *Ground instructor certificate.*

j) **Age limitation for certain operations**.

1) Age limitation. No person who holds a pilot certificate issued under this part may serve as a pilot on a civil airplane of U.S. registry in the following operations if the person has reached his or her 60th birthday

or, in the case of operations with more than one pilot, his or her 65th birthday:

i) Scheduled international air services carrying passengers in turbo-jet-powered airplanes;

ii) Scheduled international air services carrying passengers in airplanes having a passenger-seat configuration of more than nine passenger seats, excluding each crewmember seat;

iii) Nonscheduled international air transportation for compensation or hire in airplanes having a passenger-seat configuration of more than 30 passenger seats, excluding each crewmember seat; or

iv) Scheduled international air services, or nonscheduled international air transportation for compensation or hire, in airplanes having a payload capacity of more than 7,500 pounds.

2) *Definitions*.

k) *Special purpose pilot authorization*.

l) **Inspection of certificate**. Each person who holds an airman certificate, temporary document in accordance with paragraph (a)(1)(v) or (vi) of this section, medical certificate, documents establishing alternative medical qualification under part 68 of this chapter, authorization, or license required by this part must present it and their photo identification as described in paragraph (a)(2) of this section for inspection upon a request from:

1) The Administrator;

2) An authorized representative of the National Transportation Safety Board;

3) Any Federal, State, or local law enforcement officer; or

4) An authorized representative of the Transportation Security Administration.

§ 61.15 Offenses involving alcohol or drugs.

a) A conviction for the violation of any Federal or State statute relating to the growing, processing, manufacture, sale, disposition, possession, transportation, or importation of narcotic drugs, marijuana, or depressant or stimulant drugs or substances is grounds for:

1) Denial of an application for any certificate, rating, or authorization issued under this part for a period of up to 1 year after the date of final conviction; or

2) Suspension or revocation of any certificate, rating, or authorization issued under this part.

b) Committing an act prohibited by § 91.17(a) or § 91.19(a) of this chapter is grounds for:

1) Denial of an application for a certificate, rating, or authorization issued under this part for a period of up to 1 year after the date of that act; or

2) Suspension or revocation of any certificate, rating, or authorization issued under this part.

c) For the purposes of paragraphs (d), (e), and (f) of this section, a motor vehicle action means:

1) A conviction after November 29, 1990, for the violation of any Federal or State statute relating to the operation of a motor vehicle while intoxicated by alcohol or a drug, while impaired by alcohol or a drug, or while under the influence of alcohol or a drug;

2) The cancellation, suspension, or revocation of a license to operate a motor vehicle after November 29, 1990, for a cause related to the operation of a motor vehicle while intoxicated by alcohol or a drug, while impaired by alcohol or a drug, or while under the influence of alcohol or a drug; or

3) The denial after November 29, 1990, of an application for a license to operate a motor vehicle for a cause related to the operation of a

motor vehicle while intoxicated by alcohol or a drug, while impaired by alcohol or a drug, or while under the influence of alcohol or a drug.

d) Except for a motor vehicle action that results from the same incident or arises out of the same factual circumstances, a motor vehicle action occurring within 3 years of a previous motor vehicle action is grounds for:

1) Denial of an application for any certificate, rating, or authorization issued under this part for a period of up to 1 year after the date of the last motor vehicle action; or

2) Suspension or revocation of any certificate, rating, or authorization issued under this part.

e) Each person holding a certificate issued under this part shall provide a written report of each motor vehicle action to the FAA, Civil Aviation Security Division (AMC-700), P.O. Box 25810, Oklahoma City, OK 73125, not later than 60 days after the motor vehicle action. The report must include:

1) The person's name, address, date of birth, and airman certificate number;

2) The type of violation that resulted in the conviction or the administrative action;

3) The date of the conviction or administrative action;

4) The State that holds the record of conviction or administrative action; and

5) A statement of whether the motor vehicle action resulted from the same incident or arose out of the same factual circumstances related to a previously reported motor vehicle action.

f) Failure to comply with paragraph (e) of this section is grounds for:

1) Denial of an application for any certificate, rating, or authorization issued under this part for a period of up to 1 year after the date of the motor vehicle action; or

2) Suspension or revocation of any certificate, rating, or authorization issued under this part.

§ 61.16 Refusal to submit to an alcohol test or to furnish test results.

A refusal to submit to a test to indicate the percentage by weight of alcohol in the blood, when requested by a law enforcement officer in accordance with § 91.17(c) of this chapter, or a refusal to furnish or authorize the release of the test results requested by the Administrator in accordance with § 91.17(c) or (d) of this chapter, is grounds for:

a) Denial of an application for any certificate, rating, or authorization issued under this part for a period of up to 1 year after the date of that refusal; or

b) Suspension or revocation of any certificate, rating, or authorization issued under this part.

§ 61.17 Temporary certificate.

a) A temporary pilot, flight instructor, or ground instructor certificate or rating is issued for up to 120 days, at which time a permanent certificate will be issued to a person whom the Administrator finds qualified under this part.

b) A temporary pilot, flight instructor, or ground instructor certificate or rating expires:

   1) On the expiration date shown on the certificate;

   2) Upon receipt of the permanent certificate; or

   3) Upon receipt of a notice that the certificate or rating sought is denied or revoked.

§ 61.19 Duration of pilot and instructor certificates and privileges.

a) **General**.

1) The holder of a certificate with an expiration date may not, after that date, exercise the privileges of that certificate.

2) Except for a certificate issued with an expiration date, a pilot certificate is valid unless it is surrendered, suspended, or revoked.

b) *Paper student pilot certificate*.

c) **Pilot certificates**.

1) A pilot certificate (including a student pilot certificate issued after April 1, 2016 issued under this part is issued without a specific expiration date.

2) The holder of a pilot certificate issued on the basis of a foreign pilot license may exercise the privileges of that certificate only while that person's foreign pilot license is effective.

d) *Flight instructor certificate*.

e) *Ground instructor certificate*.

f) *Return of certificates*.

g) *Duration of certain pilot certificates*.

§ 61.23 Medical certificates: Requirement and duration.

a) **Operations requiring a medical certificate**. Except as provided in paragraphs (b) and (c) of this section, a person–

1) Must hold a first-class medical certificate:

i) *PIC ATP privileges*;

ii) *SIC ATP privileges*; or

iii) *Part 121 crew, 60 yrs and older*.

2) Must hold at least a second class medical certificate when exercising:

i) *SIC Part 121, any age*; or

ii) Privileges of a commercial pilot certificate; or

3) Must hold at least a third-class medical certificate–

i) *Private pilot privileges*;

ii) *PIC CFI privileges*;

iii) When taking a practical test in an aircraft for a recreational pilot, private pilot, commercial pilot, or airline transport pilot certificate, or for a flight instructor certificate, except when operating under the conditions and limitations set forth in § 61.113(i); or

iv) *Examiner privileges*.

b) *Operations not requiring a medical certificate.*

c) *Operations requiring either a medical certificate or U.S. driver's license.*

d) **Duration of a medical certificate**. Use the following table to determine duration for each class of medical certificate:

(the following table is abbreviated for formatting and ease of reading)

If you hold	And on the medical date, you were	And you are conducting an operation requiring	Then your medical expires, for that operation, at the end of the last day of the month after the
(1) A first-class medical	(i) Under 40	*ATP PIC or SIC Part 121 privileges*	12th month after exam date
	(ii) 40 or older	*ATP PIC, SIC Part 121, or Part 121 (after 60th b-day) privileges*	6th month after exam date
	(iii) Any age	*Commercial pilot or ATC privileges*	12th month after exam date
	(iv) Under 40	*Private, CFI (PIC), or student privileges*	60th month after exam date
	(v) 40 or older	*Private, CFI (PIC), or student privileges*	24th month after exam date
(2) A second-class medical	(i) Any age	*ATP SIC, commercial pilot, or ATC privileges*	12th month after exam date
	(ii) Under 40	*Private, CFI (PIC), or student privileges*	60th month after exam date
	(iii) 40 or older	*Private, CFI (PIC), or student privileges*	24th month after exam date
(3) A third-class medical	(i) Under 40	*Private, CFI (PIC), or student privileges*	60th month after exam date
	(ii) 40 or older	*Private, CFI (PIC), or student privileges*	24th month after exam date

§ 61.29 Replacement of a lost or destroyed airman or medical certificate or knowledge test report.

a) A request for the replacement of a lost or destroyed airman certificate issued under this part must be made:

1) By letter to the Department of Transportation, FAA, Airmen Certification Branch, P.O. Box 25082, Oklahoma City, OK 73125, and must be

accompanied by a check or money order for the appropriate fee payable to the FAA; or

2) In any other manner and form approved by the Administrator including a request online to Airmen Services at http://www.faa.gov, and must be accompanied by acceptable form of payment for the appropriate fee.

b) A request for the replacement of a lost or destroyed medical certificate must be made:

1) By letter to the Department of Transportation, FAA, Aerospace Medical Certification Division, P.O. Box 26200, Oklahoma City, OK 73125, and must be accompanied by a check or money order for the appropriate fee payable to the FAA; or

2) In any other manner and form approved by the Administrator and must be accompanied by acceptable form of payment for the appropriate fee.

c) A request for the replacement of a lost or destroyed knowledge test report must be made:

1) By letter to the Department of Transportation, FAA, Airmen Certification Branch, P.O. Box 25082, Oklahoma City, OK 73125, and must be accompanied by a check or money order for the appropriate fee payable to the FAA; or

2) In any other manner and form approved by the Administrator and must be accompanied by acceptable form of payment for the appropriate fee.

d) The letter requesting replacement of a lost or destroyed airman certificate, medical certificate, or knowledge test report must state:

1) The name of the person;

2) The permanent mailing address (including ZIP code), or if the permanent mailing address includes a post office box number, then the person's current residential address;

3) The certificate holder's date and place of birth; and

4) Any information regarding the–

i) Grade, number, and date of issuance of the airman certificate and ratings, if appropriate;

ii) Class of medical certificate, the place and date of the medical exam, name of the Airman Medical Examiner (AME), and the circumstances concerning the loss of the original medical certificate, as appropriate; and

iii) Date the knowledge test was taken, if appropriate.

e) A person who has lost an airman certificate, medical certificate, or knowledge test report may obtain, in a form or manner approved by the Administrator, a document conveying temporary authority to exercise certificate privileges from the FAA Aeromedical Certification Branch or the Airman Certification Branch, as appropriate, and the:

1) Document may be carried as an airman certificate, medical certificate, or knowledge test report, as appropriate, for up to 60 days pending the person's receipt of a duplicate under paragraph (a), (b), or (c) of this section, unless the person has been notified that the certificate has been suspended or revoked.

2) Request for such a document must include the date on which a duplicate certificate or knowledge test report was previously requested.

§ 61.31 Type rating requirements, additional training, and authorization requirements.

a) **Type ratings required**. A person who acts as a pilot in command of any of the following aircraft must hold a type rating for that aircraft:

1) Large aircraft (except lighter-than-air).

2) Turbojet-powered airplanes.

3) Other aircraft specified by the Administrator through aircraft type certificate procedures.

b) *Authorization in lieu of a type rating*.

c) **Aircraft category, class, and type ratings**: Limitations on the carriage of persons, or operating for compensation or hire. Unless a person holds a category, class, and type rating (if a class and type rating is required) that applies to the aircraft, that person may not act as pilot in command of an aircraft that is carrying another person, or is operated for compensation or hire. That person also may not act as pilot in command of that aircraft for compensation or hire.

d) **Aircraft category, class, and type ratings: Limitations on operating an aircraft as the pilot in command**. To serve as the pilot in command of an aircraft, a person must–

1) Hold the appropriate category, class, and type rating (if a class or type rating is required) for the aircraft to be flown; or

2) Have received training required by this part that is appropriate to the pilot certification level, aircraft category, class, and type rating (if a class or type rating is required) for the aircraft to be flown, and have received an endorsement for solo flight in that aircraft from an authorized instructor.

e) **Additional training required for operating complex airplanes**.

1) Except as provided in paragraph (e)(2) of this section, no person may act as pilot in command of a complex airplane, unless the person has–

i) Received and logged ground and flight training from an authorized instructor in a complex airplane, or in a full flight simulator or flight training device that is representative of a complex airplane, and has been found proficient in the operation and systems of the airplane; and

ii) Received a one-time endorsement in the pilot's logbook from an authorized instructor who certifies the person is proficient to operate a complex airplane.

2) *Historical (pre-1997) and Part 135 exceptions*.

f) **Additional training required for operating high-performance airplanes**.

1) Except as provided in paragraph (f)(2) of this section, no person may act as pilot in command of a high-performance airplane (an airplane with an engine of more than 200 horsepower), unless the person has–

i) Received and logged ground and flight training from an authorized instructor in a high-performance airplane, or in a full flight simulator or flight training device that is representative of a high-performance airplane, and has been found proficient in the operation and systems of the airplane; and

ii) Received a one-time endorsement in the pilot's logbook from an authorized instructor who certifies the person is proficient to operate a high-performance airplane.

2) *Historical (pre-1997) and Part 135 exceptions*.

g) **Additional training required for operating pressurized aircraft capable of operating at high altitudes**.

1) Except as provided in paragraph (g)(3) of this section, no person may act as pilot in command of a pressurized aircraft (an aircraft that has a service ceiling or maximum operating altitude, whichever is lower, above 25,000 feet MSL), unless that person has received and logged ground training from an authorized instructor and obtained an endorsement in the person's logbook or training record from an authorized instructor who certifies the person has satisfactorily accomplished the ground training. The ground training must include at least the following subjects:

i) High-altitude aerodynamics and meteorology;

ii) Respiration;

iii) Effects, symptoms, and causes of hypoxia and any other high-altitude sickness;

iv) Duration of consciousness without supplemental oxygen;

v) Effects of prolonged usage of supplemental oxygen;

vi) Causes and effects of gas expansion and gas bubble formation;

vii) Preventive measures for eliminating gas expansion, gas bubble formation, and high-altitude sickness;

viii) Physical phenomena and incidents of decompression; and

ix) Any other physiological aspects of high-altitude flight.

2) Except as provided in paragraph (g)(3) of this section, no person may act as pilot in command of a pressurized aircraft unless that person has received and logged training from an authorized instructor in a pressurized aircraft, or in a full flight simulator or flight training device that is representative of a pressurized aircraft, and obtained an endorsement in the person's logbook or training record from an authorized instructor who found the person proficient in the operation of a pressurized aircraft. The flight training must include at least the following subjects:

i) Normal cruise flight operations while operating above 25,000 feet MSL;

ii) Proper emergency procedures for simulated rapid decompression without actually depressurizing the aircraft; and

iii) Emergency descent procedures.

3) *Historical (pre-1991), military, and Part 135 exceptions.*

h) **Additional aircraft type-specific training**. No person may serve as pilot in command of an aircraft that the Administrator has determined requires aircraft type-specific training unless that person has–

1) Received and logged type-specific training in the aircraft, or in a full flight simulator or flight training device that is representative of that type of aircraft; and

2) Received a logbook endorsement from an authorized instructor who has found the person proficient in the operation of the aircraft and its systems.

i) **Additional training required for operating tailwheel airplanes**.

1) Except as provided in paragraph (i)(2) of this section, no person may act as pilot in command of a tailwheel airplane unless that person has received and logged flight training from an authorized instructor in a tailwheel airplane and received an endorsement in the person's logbook from an authorized instructor who found the person proficient in the operation of a tailwheel airplane. The flight training must include at least the following maneuvers and procedures:

i) Normal and crosswind takeoffs and landings;

ii) Wheel landings (unless the manufacturer has recommended against such landings); and

iii) Go-around procedures.

2) The training and endorsement required by paragraph (i)(1) of this section is not required if the person logged pilot-in-command time in a tailwheel airplane before April 15, 1991.

j) *Additional training required for operating a glider.*

k) *Additional training required for night vision goggle operations.*

l) **Exceptions**.

1) This section does not require a category and class rating for aircraft not type-certificated as airplanes, rotorcraft, gliders, lighter-than-air aircraft, powered-lifts, powered parachutes, or weight-shift-control aircraft.

2) The rating limitations of this section do not apply to–

i) An applicant when taking a practical test given by an examiner;

ii) *The holder of a student pilot certificate;*

iii) *Certain provisional and experimental operations;*

iv) *Certain balloon operations;*

v) *Certain recreational pilot operations;* or

vi) *Certain sport pilot operations.*

§ 61.39 Prerequisites for practical tests.

a) Except as provided in paragraphs (b), (c), and (e) of this section, to be eligible for a practical test for a certificate or rating issued under this part, an applicant must:

1) Pass the required knowledge test:

i) Within the 24-calendar-month period preceding the month the applicant completes the practical test, if a knowledge test is required; or

ii) Within the 60-calendar month period preceding the month the applicant completes the practical test for those applicants who complete the airline transport pilot certification training program in § 61.156 and pass the knowledge test for an airline transport pilot certificate with a multiengine class rating after July 31, 2014;

2) Present the knowledge test report at the time of application for the practical test, if a knowledge test is required;

3) Have satisfactorily accomplished the required training and obtained the aeronautical experience prescribed by this part for the certificate or rating sought, and if applying for the practical test with flight time accomplished under § 61.159(c), present a copy of the records required by § 135.63(a)(4)(vi) and (x) of this chapter;

4) Hold at least a third-class medical certificate, if a medical certificate is required;

5) Meet the prescribed age requirement of this part for the issuance of the certificate or rating sought;

6) Have an endorsement, if required by this part, in the applicant's logbook or training record that has been signed by an authorized instructor who certifies that the applicant–

i) Has received and logged training time within 2 calendar months preceding the month of application in preparation for the practical test;

ii) Is prepared for the required practical test; and

iii) Has demonstrated satisfactory knowledge of the subject areas in which the applicant was deficient on the airman knowledge test; and

7) Have a completed and signed application form.

b) *Airline transport pilots.*

c) *Airline transport pilots.*

d) *Airline transport pilots.*

e) A person is not required to comply with the provisions of paragraph (a)(6) of this section if that person:

1) Holds a foreign pilot license issued by a contracting State to the Convention on International Civil Aviation that authorizes at least the privileges of the pilot certificate sought;

2) *Type ratings*; or

3) *Airline transport pilots.*

f) If all increments of the practical test for a certificate or rating are not completed on the same date, then all the remaining increments of the test must be completed within 2 calendar months after the month the applicant began the test.

g) If all increments of the practical test for a certificate or rating are not completed within 2 calendar months after the month the applicant began the test, the applicant must retake the entire practical test.

§ 61.51 Pilot logbooks.

a) **Training time and aeronautical experience**. Each person must document and record the following time in a manner acceptable to the Administrator:

1) Training and aeronautical experience used to meet the requirements for a certificate, rating, or flight review of this part.

2) The aeronautical experience required for meeting the recent flight experience requirements of this part.

b) **Logbook entries**. For the purposes of meeting the requirements of paragraph (a) of this section, each person must enter the following information for each flight or lesson logged:

1) General–

i) Date.

ii) Total flight time or lesson time.

iii) Location where the aircraft departed and arrived, or for lessons in a full flight simulator or flight training device, the location where the lesson occurred.

iv) Type and identification of aircraft, full flight simulator, flight training device, or aviation training device, as appropriate.

v) The name of a safety pilot, if required by § 91.109 of this chapter.

2) Type of pilot experience or training–

i) Solo.

ii) Pilot in command.

iii) Second in command.

iv) Flight and ground training received from an authorized instructor.

v) Training received in a full flight simulator, flight training device, or aviation training device from an authorized instructor.

3) Conditions of flight–

i) Day or night.

ii) Actual instrument.

iii) Simulated instrument conditions in flight, a full flight simulator, flight training device, or aviation training device.

iv) *Use of night vision goggles*.

c) **Logging of pilot time**. The pilot time described in this section may be used to:

1) Apply for a certificate or rating issued under this part or a privilege authorized under this part; or

2) Satisfy the recent flight experience requirements of this part.

d) *Logging of solo flight time.*

e) **Logging pilot-in-command flight time**.

1) A sport, recreational, private, commercial, or airline transport pilot may log pilot in command flight time for flights-

i) Except when logging flight time under § 61.159(c), when the pilot is the sole manipulator of the controls of an aircraft for which the pilot is rated, or has sport pilot privileges for that category and class of aircraft, if the aircraft class rating is appropriate;

ii) When the pilot is the sole occupant in the aircraft;

iii) When the pilot, except for a holder of a sport or recreational pilot certificate, acts as pilot in command of an aircraft for which more than one pilot is required under the type certification of the aircraft or the regulations under which the flight is conducted; or

iv) *Under the supervision of a qualified pilot in command.*

2) *Airline transport pilots.*

3) *Certificated flight instructors.*

4) *Student pilots.*

5) A commercial pilot or airline transport pilot may log all flight time while acting as pilot in command of an operation in accordance with § 135.99(c) of this chapter if the flight is conducted in accordance with an approved second-in-command professional development program that meets the requirements of § 135.99(c) of this chapter.

f) **Logging second-in-command flight time**. A person may log second-in-command time only for that flight time during which that person:

1) Is qualified in accordance with the second-in-command require-ments of § 61.55, and occupies a crewmember station in an aircraft that requires more than one pilot by the aircraft's type certificate;

2) Holds the appropriate category, class, and instrument rating (if an instrument rating is required for the flight) for the aircraft being flown, and more than one pilot is required under the type certification of the aircraft or the regulations under which the flight is being conducted; or

3) *Certain operations under Part 135.*

g) **Logging instrument time**.

1) A person may log instrument time only for that flight time when the person operates the aircraft solely by reference to instruments under actual or simulated instrument flight conditions.

2) An authorized instructor may log instrument time when conducting instrument flight instruction in actual instrument flight conditions.

3) For the purposes of logging instrument time to meet the recent in-strument experience requirements of § 61.57(c) of this part, the follow-ing information must be recorded in the person's logbook–

i) The location and type of each instrument approach accomplished; and

ii) The name of the safety pilot, if required.

4) A person may use time in a full flight simulator, flight training device, or aviation training device for acquiring instrument aeronautical expe-rience for a pilot certificate or rating provided an authorized instructor is present to observe that time and signs the person's logbook or train-ing record to verify the time and the content of the training session.

5) A person may use time in a full flight simulator, flight training device, or aviation training device for satisfying instrument recency experi-ence requirements provided a logbook or training record is main-tained to specify the training device, time, and the content.

h) **Logging training time**.

1) A person may log training time when that person receives training from an authorized instructor in an aircraft, full flight simulator, flight training device, or aviation training device.

2) The training time must be logged in a logbook and must:

i) Be endorsed in a legible manner by the authorized instructor; and

ii) Include a description of the training given, the length of the training lesson, and the authorized instructor's signature, certificate number, and certificate expiration date.

i) **Presentation of required documents**.

1) Persons must present their pilot certificate, medical certificate, logbook, or any other record required by this part for inspection upon a reasonable request by–

i) The Administrator;

ii) An authorized representative from the National Transportation Safety Board; or

iii) Any Federal, State, or local law enforcement officer.

2) *Student pilots*.

3) *Sport pilots*.

4) *Recreational pilots*.

5) *Certain flight instructors*.

j) **Aircraft requirements for logging flight time**. For a person to log flight time, the time must be acquired in an aircraft that is identified as an aircraft under § 61.5(b), and is–

1) An aircraft of U.S. registry with either a standard or special airworthiness certificate;

2) *Foreign registry*;

3) *A military aircraft*; or

4) *A public aircraft*.

k) *Logging night vision goggle time.*

§ 61.56 Flight review.

a) Except as provided in paragraphs (b) and (f) of this section, a flight review consists of a minimum of 1 hour of flight training and 1 hour of ground training. The review must include:

1) A review of the current general operating and flight rules of part 91 of this chapter; and

2) A review of those maneuvers and procedures that, at the discretion of the person giving the review, are necessary for the pilot to demonstrate the safe exercise of the privileges of the pilot certificate.

b) *Glider pilots.*

c) Except as provided in paragraphs (d), (e), and (g) of this section, no person may act as pilot in command of an aircraft unless, since the beginning of the 24th calendar month before the month in which that pilot acts as pilot in command, that person has–

1) Accomplished a flight review given in an aircraft for which that pilot is rated by an authorized instructor and

2) A logbook endorsed from an authorized instructor who gave the review certifying that the person has satisfactorily completed the review.

d) A person who has, within the period specified in paragraph (c) of this section, passed any of the following need not accomplish the flight review required by this section:

1) A pilot proficiency check or practical test conducted by an examiner, an approved pilot check airman, or a U.S. Armed Force, for a pilot certificate, rating, or operating privilege.

2) A practical test conducted by an examiner for the issuance of a flight instructor certificate, an additional rating on a flight instructor certificate, renewal of a flight instructor certificate, or reinstatement of a flight instructor certificate.

e) A person who has, within the period specified in paragraph (c) of this section, satisfactorily accomplished one or more phases of an FAA-sponsored pilot proficiency award program need not accomplish the flight review required by this section.

f) A person who holds a flight instructor certificate and who has, within the period specified in paragraph (c) of this section, satisfactorily completed a renewal of a flight instructor certificate under the provisions in § 61.197 need not accomplish the one hour of ground training specified in paragraph (a) of this section.

g) *Student pilots*.

h) The requirements of this section may be accomplished in combination with the requirements of § 61.57 and other applicable recent experience requirements at the discretion of the authorized instructor conducting the flight review.

i) A flight simulator or flight training device may be used to meet the flight review requirements of this section subject to the following conditions:

1) The flight simulator or flight training device must be used in accordance with an approved course conducted by a training center certificated under part 142 of this chapter.

2) Unless the flight review is undertaken in a flight simulator that is approved for landings, the applicant must meet the takeoff and landing requirements of § 61.57(a) or § 61.57(b) of this part.

3) The flight simulator or flight training device used must represent an aircraft or set of aircraft for which the pilot is rated.

§ 61.57 Recent flight experience: Pilot in command.

a) **General experience**.

1) Except as provided in paragraph (e) of this section, no person may act as a pilot in command of an aircraft carrying passengers or of an aircraft certificated for more than one pilot flight crewmember unless

that person has made at least three takeoffs and three landings within the preceding 90 days, and–

i) The person acted as the sole manipulator of the flight controls; and

ii) The required takeoffs and landings were performed in an aircraft of the same category, class, and type (if a type rating is required), and, if the aircraft to be flown is an airplane with a tailwheel, the takeoffs and landings must have been made to a full stop in an airplane with a tailwheel.

2) For the purpose of meeting the requirements of paragraph (a)(1) of this section, a person may act as a pilot in command of an aircraft under day VFR or day IFR, provided no persons or property are carried on board the aircraft, other than those necessary for the conduct of the flight.

3) The takeoffs and landings required by paragraph (a)(1) of this section may be accomplished in a full flight simulator or flight training device that is–

i) Approved by the Administrator for landings; and

ii) Used in accordance with an approved course conducted by a training center certificated under part 142 of this chapter.

b) **Night takeoff and landing experience**.

1) Except as provided in paragraph (e) of this section, no person may act as pilot in command of an aircraft carrying passengers during the period beginning 1 hour after sunset and ending 1 hour before sunrise, unless within the preceding 90 days that person has made at least three takeoffs and three landings to a full stop during the period beginning 1 hour after sunset and ending 1 hour before sunrise, and–

i) That person acted as sole manipulator of the flight controls; and

ii) The required takeoffs and landings were performed in an aircraft of the same category, class, and type (if a type rating is required).

2) The takeoffs and landings required by paragraph (b)(1) of this section may be accomplished in a full flight simulator that is–

i) Approved by the Administrator for takeoffs and landings, if the visual system is adjusted to represent the period described in paragraph (b)(1) of this section; and

ii) Used in accordance with an approved course conducted by a training center certificated under part 142 of this chapter.

c) **Instrument experience**. Except as provided in paragraph (e) of this section, a person may act as pilot in command under IFR or weather conditions less than the minimums prescribed for VFR only if:

1) **Use of an airplane, powered-lift, helicopter, or airship for maintaining instrument experience**. Within the 6 calendar months preceding the month of the flight, that person performed and logged at least the following tasks and iterations in an airplane, powered-lift, helicopter, or airship, as appropriate, for the instrument rating privileges to be maintained in actual weather conditions, or under simulated conditions using a view-limiting device that involves having performed the following–

i) Six instrument approaches.

ii) Holding procedures and tasks.

iii) Intercepting and tracking courses through the use of navigational electronic systems.

2) **Use of a full flight simulator, flight training device, or aviation training device for maintaining instrument experience**. A pilot may accomplish the requirements in paragraph (c)(1) of this section in a full flight simulator, flight training device, or aviation training device provided the device represents the category of aircraft for the instrument rating privileges to be maintained and the pilot performs the tasks and iterations in simulated instrument conditions. A person may complete the instrument experience in any combination of an aircraft, full flight simulator, flight training device, or aviation training device.

3) *Maintaining instrument recent experience in a glider*.

d) **Instrument proficiency check**.

1) Except as provided in paragraph (e) of this section, a person who has failed to meet the instrument experience requirements of paragraph (c) of this section for more than six calendar months may reestablish instrument currency only by completing an instrument proficiency check. The instrument proficiency check must consist of at least the following areas of operation:

i) Air traffic control clearances and procedures;

ii) Flight by reference to instruments;

iii) Navigation systems;

iv) Instrument approach procedures;

v) Emergency operations; and

vi) Postflight procedures.

2) The instrument proficiency check must be–

i) In an aircraft that is appropriate to the aircraft category;

ii) For other than a glider, in a full flight simulator or flight training device that is representative of the aircraft category; or

iii) *For gliders.*

3) The instrument proficiency check must be given by–

i) An examiner;

ii) *A person authorized by the U.S. Armed Forces;*

iii) *A company check pilot;*

iv) An authorized instructor; or

v) A person approved by the Administrator to conduct instrument practical tests.

e) *Exceptions.*

f) *Night vision goggle operating experience.*

g) *Night vision goggle proficiency check.*

§ 61.60 Change of address.

The holder of a pilot, flight instructor, or ground instructor certificate who has made a change in permanent mailing address may not, after 30 days from that date, exercise the privileges of the certificate unless the holder has notified in writing the FAA, Airman Certification Branch, P.O. Box 25082, Oklahoma City, OK 73125, of the new permanent mailing address, or if the permanent mailing address includes a post office box number, then the holder's current residential address.

§ 61.63 Additional aircraft ratings (other than for ratings at the airline transport pilot certification level).

a) **General**. For an additional aircraft rating on a pilot certificate, other than for an airline transport pilot certificate, a person must meet the requirements of this section appropriate to the additional aircraft rating sought.

b) **Additional aircraft category rating**. A person who applies to add a category rating to a pilot certificate:

   1) Must complete the training and have the applicable aeronautical experience.

   2) Must have a logbook or training record endorsement from an authorized instructor attesting that the person was found competent in the appropriate aeronautical knowledge areas and proficient in the appropriate areas of operation.

   3) Must pass the practical test.

   4) Need not take an additional knowledge test, provided the applicant holds an airplane, rotorcraft, powered-lift, weight-shift-control aircraft, powered parachute, or airship rating at that pilot certificate level.

c) **Additional aircraft class rating**. A person who applies for an additional class rating on a pilot certificate:

1) Must have a logbook or training record endorsement from an authorized instructor attesting that the person was found competent in the appropriate aeronautical knowledge areas and proficient in the appropriate areas of operation.

2) Must pass the practical test.

3) Need not meet the specified training time requirements prescribed by this part that apply to the pilot certificate for the aircraft class rating sought; unless, the person only holds a lighter-than-air category rating with a balloon class rating and is seeking an airship class rating, then that person must receive the specified training time requirements and possess the appropriate aeronautical experience.

4) Need not take an additional knowledge test, provided the applicant holds an airplane, rotorcraft, powered-lift, weight-shift-control aircraft, powered parachute, or airship rating at that pilot certificate level.

d) **Additional aircraft type rating**. Except as provided under paragraph (d)(6) of this section, a person who applies for an aircraft type rating or an aircraft type rating to be completed concurrently with an aircraft category or class rating–

1) Must hold or concurrently obtain an appropriate instrument rating, except as provided in paragraph (e) of this section.

2) Must have a logbook or training record endorsement from an authorized instructor attesting that the person is competent in the appropriate aeronautical knowledge areas and proficient in the appropriate areas of operation at the airline transport pilot certification level.

3) Must pass the practical test at the airline transport pilot certification level.

4) Must perform the practical test in actual or simulated instrument conditions, except as provided in paragraph (e) of this section.

5) Need not take an additional knowledge test if the applicant holds an airplane, rotorcraft, powered-lift, or airship rating on the pilot certificate.

6) *Part 121, 135, and fractionals.*

e) *Aircraft not capable of instrument maneuvers and procedures.*

f) *Multiengine airplane with a single-pilot station.*

g) *Single engine airplane with a single-pilot station.*

h) *Experimental certificates.*

§ 61.123 Eligibility requirements: General.

To be eligible for a commercial pilot certificate, a person must:

a) Be at least 18 years of age;

b) Be able to read, speak, write, and understand the English language. If the applicant is unable to meet one of these requirements due to medical reasons, then the Administrator may place such operating limitations on that applicant's pilot certificate as are necessary for the safe operation of the aircraft.

c) Receive a logbook endorsement from an authorized instructor who:

1) Conducted the required ground training or reviewed the person's home study on the aeronautical knowledge areas listed in § 61.125 of this part that apply to the aircraft category and class rating sought; and

2) Certified that the person is prepared for the required knowledge test that applies to the aircraft category and class rating sought.

d) Pass the required knowledge test on the aeronautical knowledge areas listed in § 61.125 of this part;

e) Receive the required training and a logbook endorsement from an authorized instructor who:

1) Conducted the training on the areas of operation listed in § 61.127(b) of this part that apply to the aircraft category and class rating sought; and

2) Certified that the person is prepared for the required practical test.

f) Meet the aeronautical experience requirements of this subpart that apply to the aircraft category and class rating sought before applying for the practical test;

g) Pass the required practical test on the areas of operation listed in § 61.127(b) of this part that apply to the aircraft category and class rating sought;

h) Hold at least a private pilot certificate issued under this part or meet the requirements of § 61.73; and

i) Comply with the sections of this part that apply to the aircraft category and class rating sought.

§ 61.125 Aeronautical knowledge.

a) **General**. A person who applies for a commercial pilot certificate must receive and log ground training from an authorized instructor, or complete a home-study course, on the aeronautical knowledge areas of paragraph (b) of this section that apply to the aircraft category and class rating sought.

b) **Aeronautical knowledge areas**.

1) Applicable Federal Aviation Regulations of this chapter that relate to commercial pilot privileges, limitations, and flight operations;

2) Accident reporting requirements of the National Transportation Safety Board;

3) Basic aerodynamics and the principles of flight;

4) Meteorology to include recognition of critical weather situations, windshear recognition and avoidance, and the use of aeronautical weather reports and forecasts;

5) Safe and efficient operation of aircraft;

6) Weight and balance computations;

7) Use of performance charts;

8) Significance and effects of exceeding aircraft performance limitations;

9) Use of aeronautical charts and a magnetic compass for pilotage and dead reckoning;

10) Use of air navigation facilities;

11) Aeronautical decision making and judgment;

12) Principles and functions of aircraft systems;

13) Maneuvers, procedures, and emergency operations appropriate to the aircraft;

14) Night and high-altitude operations;

15) Procedures for operating within the National Airspace System; and

16) *Lighter-than-air ratings*.

§ 61.127 Flight proficiency.

a) **General**. A person who applies for a commercial pilot certificate must receive and log ground and flight training from an authorized instructor on the areas of operation of this section that apply to the aircraft category and class rating sought.

b) **Areas of operation**.

1) For an airplane category rating with a single-engine class rating:

i) Preflight preparation;

ii) Preflight procedures;

iii) Airport and seaplane base operations;

iv) Takeoffs, landings, and go-arounds;

v) Performance maneuvers;

vi) Ground reference maneuvers;

vii) Navigation;

viii) Slow flight and stalls;

ix) Emergency operations;

x) High-altitude operations; and

xi) Postflight procedures.

2) For an airplane category rating with a multiengine class rating:

i) Preflight preparation;

ii) Preflight procedures;

iii) Airport and seaplane base operations;

iv) Takeoffs, landings, and go-arounds;

v) Performance maneuvers;

vi) Navigation;

vii) Slow flight and stalls;

viii) Emergency operations;

ix) Multiengine operations;

x) High-altitude operations; and

xi) Postflight procedures.

3) *For a rotorcraft category rating with a helicopter class rating.*

4) *For a rotorcraft category rating with a gyroplane class rating.*

5) *For a powered-lift category rating.*

6) *For a glider category rating.*

7) *For a lighter-than-air category rating with an airship class rating.*

8) *For a lighter-than-air category rating with a balloon class rating.*

§ 61.129 Aeronautical experience.

a) **For an airplane single-engine rating**. Except as provided in paragraph (i) of this section, a person who applies for a commercial pilot certificate with an airplane category and single-engine class rating must log at least 250 hours of flight time as a pilot that consists of at least:

1) 100 hours in powered aircraft, of which 50 hours must be in airplanes.

2) 100 hours of pilot-in-command flight time, which includes at least–

i) 50 hours in airplanes; and

ii) 50 hours in cross-country flight of which at least 10 hours must be in airplanes.

3) 20 hours of training on the areas of operation listed in § 61.127(b)(1) of this part that includes at least–

i) Ten hours of instrument training using a view-limiting device including attitude instrument flying, partial panel skills, recovery from unusual flight attitudes, and intercepting and tracking navigational systems. Five hours of the 10 hours required on instrument training must be in a single engine airplane;

ii) 10 hours of training in a complex airplane, a turbine-powered airplane, or a technically advanced airplane (TAA) that meets the requirements of paragraph (j) of this section, or any combination thereof. The airplane must be appropriate to land or sea for the rating sought;

iii) One 2-hour cross country flight in a single engine airplane in daytime conditions that consists of a total straight-line distance of more than 100 nautical miles from the original point of departure;

iv) One 2-hour cross country flight in a single engine airplane in nighttime conditions that consists of a total straight-line distance of more than 100 nautical miles from the original point of departure; and

v) Three hours in a single-engine airplane with an authorized instructor in preparation for the practical test within the preceding 2 calendar months from the month of the test.

4) Ten hours of solo flight time in a single engine airplane or 10 hours of flight time performing the duties of pilot in command in a single engine airplane with an authorized instructor on board (either of which may be credited towards the flight time requirement under paragraph (a)(2) of this section), on the areas of operation listed under § 61.127(b)(1) that include–

i) One cross-country flight of not less than 300 nautical miles total distance, with landings at a minimum of three points, one of which is a straight-line distance of at least 250 nautical miles from the original departure point. However, if this requirement is being met in Hawaii, the longest segment need only have a straight-line distance of at least 150 nautical miles; and

ii) 5 hours in night VFR conditions with 10 takeoffs and 10 landings (with each landing involving a flight in the traffic pattern) at an airport with an operating control tower.

b) **For an airplane multiengine rating**. Except as provided in paragraph (i) of this section, a person who applies for a commercial pilot certificate with an airplane category and multiengine class rating must log at least 250 hours of flight time as a pilot that consists of at least:

1) 100 hours in powered aircraft, of which 50 hours must be in airplanes.

2) 100 hours of pilot-in-command flight time, which includes at least–

i) 50 hours in airplanes; and

ii) 50 hours in cross-country flight of which at least 10 hours must be in airplanes.

3) 20 hours of training on the areas of operation listed in § 61.127(b)(2) of this part that includes at least–

i) Ten hours of instrument training using a view-limiting device including attitude instrument flying, partial panel skills, recovery from unusual flight attitudes, and intercepting and tracking navigational systems. Five hours of the 10 hours required on instrument training must be in a multiengine airplane;

ii) 10 hours of training in a multiengine complex or turbine-powered airplane; or for an applicant seeking a multiengine seaplane rating, 10 hours of training in a multiengine seaplane that has flaps and a controllable pitch propeller, including seaplanes equipped with an engine control system consisting of a digital computer and associated accessories for controlling the engine and propeller, such as a full authority digital engine control;

iii) One 2-hour cross country flight in a multiengine airplane in daytime conditions that consists of a total straight-line distance of more than 100 nautical miles from the original point of departure;

iv) One 2-hour cross country flight in a multiengine airplane in nighttime conditions that consists of a total straight-line distance of more than 100 nautical miles from the original point of departure; and

v) Three hours in a multiengine airplane with an authorized instructor in preparation for the practical test within the preceding 2 calendar months from the month of the test.

4) 10 hours of solo flight time in a multiengine airplane or 10 hours of flight time performing the duties of pilot in command in a multiengine airplane with an authorized instructor (either of which may be credited towards the flight time requirement in paragraph (b)(2) of this section), on the areas of operation listed in § 61.127(b)(2) of this part that includes at least–

i) One cross-country flight of not less than 300 nautical miles total distance with landings at a minimum of three points, one of which is a straight-line distance of at least 250 nautical miles from the original departure point. However, if this requirement is being met in Hawaii, the longest segment need only have a straight-line distance of at least 150 nautical miles; and

ii) 5 hours in night VFR conditions with 10 takeoffs and 10 landings (with each landing involving a flight with a traffic pattern) at an airport with an operating control tower.

c) *For a helicopter rating.*

d) *For a gyroplane rating.*

e) *For a powered-lift rating.*

f) *For a glider rating.*

g) *For an airship rating.*

h) *For a balloon rating.*

i) **Permitted credit for use of a flight simulator or flight training device**.

1) Except as provided in paragraph (i)(2) of this section, an applicant who has not accomplished the training required by this section in a course conducted by a training center certificated under part 142 of this chapter may:

i) Credit a maximum of 50 hours toward the total aeronautical experience requirements for an airplane or powered-lift rating, provided the aeronautical experience was obtained from an authorized instructor in a full flight simulator or flight training device that represents that class of airplane or powered-lift category and type, if applicable, appropriate to the rating sought; and

ii) Credit a maximum of 25 hours toward the total aeronautical experience requirements of this section for a helicopter rating, provided the aeronautical experience was obtained from an authorized instructor in a full flight simulator or flight training device that represents a helicopter and type, if applicable, appropriate to the rating sought.

2) *Part 142 operations.*

3) *Part 142 exceptions.*

j) **Technically advanced airplane**. Unless otherwise authorized by the Administrator, a technically advanced airplane must be equipped with an electronically advanced avionics system that includes the following installed components:

1) An electronic Primary Flight Display (PFD) that includes, at a minimum, an airspeed indicator, turn coordinator, attitude indicator, heading indicator, altimeter, and vertical speed indicator;

2) An electronic Multifunction Display (MFD) that includes, at a minimum, a moving map using Global Positioning System (GPS) navigation with the aircraft position displayed;

3) A two axis autopilot integrated with the navigation and heading guidance system; and

4) The display elements described in paragraphs (j)(1) and (2) of this section must be continuously visible.

§ 61.133 Commercial pilot privileges and limitations.

a) **Privileges**–

1) General. A person who holds a commercial pilot certificate may act as pilot in command of an aircraft–

i) Carrying persons or property for compensation or hire, provided the person is qualified in accordance with this part and with the applicable parts of this chapter that apply to the operation; and

ii) For compensation or hire, provided the person is qualified in accordance with this part and with the applicable parts of this chapter that apply to the operation.

2) *Commercial pilots with lighter-than-air category ratings.*

b) **Limitations**.

1) A person who applies for a commercial pilot certificate with an airplane category or powered-lift category rating and does not hold an instrument rating in the same category and class will be issued a commercial pilot certificate that contains the limitation, "The carriage of passengers for hire in (airplanes) (powered-lifts) on cross-country flights in excess of 50 nautical miles or at night is prohibited." The limitation may be removed when the person satisfactorily accomplishes the requirements listed in § 61.65 of this part for an instrument rating in the same category and class of aircraft listed on the person's commercial pilot certificate.

2) *Balloon operations.*

3) *Balloon operations.*

Title 14 CFR, Part 91

General Operating and Flight Rules

§ 91.3 Responsibility and authority of the pilot in command.

a) The pilot in command of an aircraft is directly responsible for, and is the final authority as to, the operation of that aircraft.

b) In an in-flight emergency requiring immediate action, the pilot in command may deviate from any rule of this part to the extent required to meet that emergency.

c) Each pilot in command who deviates from a rule under paragraph (b) of this section shall, upon the request of the Administrator, send a written report of that deviation to the Administrator.

§ 91.7 Civil aircraft airworthiness.

a) No person may operate a civil aircraft unless it is in an airworthy condition.

b) The pilot in command of a civil aircraft is responsible for determining whether that aircraft is in condition for safe flight. The pilot in command shall discontinue the flight when unairworthy mechanical, electrical, or structural conditions occur.

§ 91.9 Civil aircraft flight manual, marking, and placard requirements.

a) Except as provided in paragraph (d) of this section, no person may operate a civil aircraft without complying with the operating limitations specified in the approved Airplane or Rotorcraft Flight Manual, markings, and placards, or as otherwise prescribed by the certificating authority of the country of registry.

b) No person may operate a U.S.-registered civil aircraft–

1) For which an Airplane or Rotorcraft Flight Manual is required by § 21.5 of this chapter unless there is available in the aircraft a current,

approved Airplane or Rotorcraft Flight Manual or the manual provided for in § 121.141(b); and

2) For which an Airplane or Rotorcraft Flight Manual is not required by § 21.5 of this chapter, unless there is available in the aircraft a current approved Airplane or Rotorcraft Flight Manual, approved manual material, markings, and placards, or any combination thereof.

c) No person may operate a U.S.-registered civil aircraft unless that aircraft is identified in accordance with part 45 of this chapter.

d) *Helicopter operations*.

§ 91.13 Careless or reckless operation.

a) **Aircraft operations for the purpose of air navigation**. No person may operate an aircraft in a careless or reckless manner so as to endanger the life or property of another.

b) **Aircraft operations other than for the purpose of air navigation**. No person may operate an aircraft, other than for the purpose of air navigation, on any part of the surface of an airport used by aircraft for air commerce (including areas used by those aircraft for receiving or discharging persons or cargo), in a careless or reckless manner so as to endanger the life or property of another.

§ 91.15 Dropping objects.

No pilot in command of a civil aircraft may allow any object to be dropped from that aircraft in flight that creates a hazard to persons or property. However, this section does not prohibit the dropping of any object if reasonable precautions are taken to avoid injury or damage to persons or property.

§ 91.17 Alcohol or drugs.

a) No person may act or attempt to act as a crewmember of a civil aircraft–

1) Within 8 hours after the consumption of any alcoholic beverage;

2) While under the influence of alcohol;

3) While using any drug that affects the person's faculties in any way contrary to safety; or

4) While having an alcohol concentration of 0.04 or greater in a blood or breath specimen. Alcohol concentration means grams of alcohol per deciliter of blood or grams of alcohol per 210 liters of breath.

b) Except in an emergency, no pilot of a civil aircraft may allow a person who appears to be intoxicated or who demonstrates by manner or physical indications that the individual is under the influence of drugs (except a medical patient under proper care) to be carried in that aircraft.

c) A crewmember shall do the following:

1) On request of a law enforcement officer, submit to a test to indicate the alcohol concentration in the blood or breath, when–

i) The law enforcement officer is authorized under State or local law to conduct the test or to have the test conducted; and

ii) The law enforcement officer is requesting submission to the test to investigate a suspected violation of State or local law governing the same or substantially similar conduct prohibited by paragraph (a)(1), (a)(2), or (a)(4) of this section.

2) Whenever the FAA has a reasonable basis to believe that a person may have violated paragraph (a)(1), (a)(2), or (a)(4) of this section, on request of the FAA, that person must furnish to the FAA the results, or authorize any clinic, hospital, or doctor, or other person to release to the FAA, the results of each test taken within 4 hours after acting or attempting to act as a crewmember that indicates an alcohol concentration in the blood or breath specimen.

d) Whenever the Administrator has a reasonable basis to believe that a person may have violated paragraph (a)(3) of this section, that person shall, upon request by the Administrator, furnish the Administrator, or authorize any clinic, hospital, doctor, or other person to release to the Administrator, the results of each test taken within 4 hours after acting or attempting to act as a crewmember that indicates the presence of any drugs in the body.

e) Any test information obtained by the Administrator under paragraph (c) or (d) of this section may be evaluated in determining a person's qualifications for any airman certificate or possible violations of this chapter and may be used as evidence in any legal proceeding under section 602, 609, or 901 of the Federal Aviation Act of 1958.

§ 91.19 Carriage of narcotic drugs, marihuana, and depressant or stimulant drugs or substances.

a) Except as provided in paragraph (b) of this section, no person may operate a civil aircraft within the United States with knowledge that narcotic drugs, marihuana, and depressant or stimulant drugs or substances as defined in Federal or State statutes are carried in the aircraft.

b) Paragraph (a) of this section does not apply to any carriage of narcotic drugs, marihuana, and depressant or stimulant drugs or substances authorized by or under any Federal or State statute or by any Federal or State agency.

§ 91.103 Preflight action.

Each pilot in command shall, before beginning a flight, become familiar with all available information concerning that flight. This information must include–

a) **For a flight under IFR or a flight not in the vicinity of an airport**, weather reports and forecasts, fuel requirements, alternatives available if the planned flight cannot be completed, and any known traffic delays of which the pilot in command has been advised by ATC;

b) **For any flight**, runway lengths at airports of intended use, and the following takeoff and landing distance information:

1) For civil aircraft for which an approved Airplane or Rotorcraft Flight Manual containing takeoff and landing distance data is required, the takeoff and landing distance data contained therein; and

2) For civil aircraft other than those specified in paragraph (b)(1) of this section, other reliable information appropriate to the aircraft, relating to aircraft performance under expected values of airport elevation and runway slope, aircraft gross weight, and wind and temperature.

§ 91.107 Use of safety belts, shoulder harnesses, and child restraint systems.

a) Unless otherwise authorized by the Administrator–

1) No pilot may take off a U.S.-registered civil aircraft (except a free balloon that incorporates a basket or gondola, or an airship type certificated before November 2, 1987) unless the pilot in command of that aircraft ensures that each person on board is briefed on how to fasten and unfasten that person's safety belt and, if installed, shoulder harness.

2) No pilot may cause to be moved on the surface, take off, or land a U.S.-registered civil aircraft (except a free balloon that incorporates a basket or gondola, or an airship type certificated before November 2, 1987) unless the pilot in command of that aircraft ensures that each person on board has been notified to fasten his or her safety belt and, if installed, his or her shoulder harness.

3) Except as provided in this paragraph, each person on board a U.S.-registered civil aircraft (except a free balloon that incorporates a basket or gondola or an airship type certificated before November 2, 1987) must occupy an approved seat or berth with a safety belt and, if installed, shoulder harness, properly secured about him or her during movement on the surface, takeoff, and landing. For seaplane and float equipped rotorcraft operations during movement on the surface, the person pushing off the seaplane or rotorcraft from the dock and the person mooring the seaplane or rotorcraft at the dock are excepted

from the preceding seating and safety belt requirements. Notwith-standing the preceding requirements of this paragraph, a person may:

i) Be held by an adult who is occupying an approved seat or berth, provided that the person being held has not reached his or her second birthday and does not occupy or use any restraining device;

ii) Use the floor of the aircraft as a seat, provided that the person is on board for the purpose of engaging in sport parachuting; or

iii) *Child restraint system provisions (read online before flights using child restraint systems).*

b) *Part 121, 125, 135, and crewmember exceptions.*

§ 91.111 Operating near other aircraft.

a) No person may operate an aircraft so close to another aircraft as to create a collision hazard.

b) No person may operate an aircraft in formation flight except by arrangement with the pilot in command of each aircraft in the formation.

c) No person may operate an aircraft, carrying passengers for hire, in formation flight.

§ 91.113 Right-of-way rules: Except water operations.

a) **Inapplicability**. This section does not apply to the operation of an aircraft on water.

b) **General**. When weather conditions permit, regardless of whether an operation is conducted under instrument flight rules or visual flight rules, vigilance shall be maintained by each person operating an aircraft so as to see and avoid other aircraft. When a rule of this section gives another aircraft the right-of-way, the pilot shall give way to that aircraft and may not pass over, under, or ahead of it unless well clear.

c) **In distress**. An aircraft in distress has the right-of-way over all other air traffic.

d) **Converging**. When aircraft of the same category are converging at approximately the same altitude (except head-on, or nearly so), the aircraft to the other's right has the right-of-way. If the aircraft are of different categories–

1) A balloon has the right-of-way over any other category of aircraft;

2) A glider has the right-of-way over an airship, powered parachute, weight-shift-control aircraft, airplane, or rotorcraft.

3) An airship has the right-of-way over a powered parachute, weight-shift-control aircraft, airplane, or rotorcraft.

However, an aircraft towing or refueling other aircraft has the right-of-way over all other engine-driven aircraft.

e) **Approaching head-on**. When aircraft are approaching each other head-on, or nearly so, each pilot of each aircraft shall alter course to the right.

f) **Overtaking**. Each aircraft that is being overtaken has the right-of-way and each pilot of an overtaking aircraft shall alter course to the right to pass well clear.

g) **Landing**. Aircraft, while on final approach to land or while landing, have the right-of-way over other aircraft in flight or operating on the surface, except that they shall not take advantage of this rule to force an aircraft off the runway surface which has already landed and is attempting to make way for an aircraft on final approach. When two or more aircraft are approaching an airport for the purpose of landing, the aircraft at the lower altitude has the right-of-way, but it shall not take advantage of this rule to cut in front of another which is on final approach to land or to overtake that aircraft.

§ 91.117 Aircraft speed.

a) Unless otherwise authorized by the Administrator, no person may operate an aircraft below 10,000 feet MSL at an indicated airspeed of more than 250 knots (288 m.p.h.).

b) Unless otherwise authorized or required by ATC, no person may operate an aircraft at or below 2,500 feet above the surface within 4 nautical miles of the primary airport of a Class C or Class D airspace area at an indicated airspeed of more than 200 knots (230 mph.). This paragraph (b) does not apply to any operations within a Class B airspace area. Such operations shall comply with paragraph (a) of this section.

c) No person may operate an aircraft in the airspace underlying a Class B airspace area designated for an airport or in a VFR corridor designated through such a Class B airspace area, at an indicated airspeed of more than 200 knots (230 mph).

d) If the minimum safe airspeed for any particular operation is greater than the maximum speed prescribed in this section, the aircraft may be operated at that minimum speed.

§ 91.119 Minimum safe altitudes: General.

Except when necessary for takeoff or landing, no person may operate an aircraft below the following altitudes:

a) **Anywhere**. An altitude allowing, if a power unit fails, an emergency landing without undue hazard to persons or property on the surface.

b) **Over congested areas**. Over any congested area of a city, town, or settlement, or over any open air assembly of persons, an altitude of 1,000 feet above the highest obstacle within a horizontal radius of 2,000 feet of the aircraft.

c) **Over other than congested areas**. An altitude of 500 feet above the surface, except over open water or sparsely populated areas. In those cases, the aircraft may not be operated closer than 500 feet to any person, vessel, vehicle, or structure.

d) *Helicopters, powered parachutes, and weight-shift-control aircraft.*

§ 91.121 Altimeter settings.

a) Each person operating an aircraft shall maintain the cruising altitude or flight level of that aircraft, as the case may be, by reference to an altimeter that is set, when operating–

1) Below 18,000 feet MSL, to–

i) The current reported altimeter setting of a station along the route and within 100 nautical miles of the aircraft;

ii) If there is no station within the area prescribed in paragraph (a)(1)(i) of this section, the current reported altimeter setting of an appropriate available station; or

iii) In the case of an aircraft not equipped with a radio, the elevation of the departure airport or an appropriate altimeter setting available before departure; or

2) At or above 18,000 feet MSL, to 29.92" Hg.

b) The lowest usable flight level is determined by the atmospheric pressure in the area of operation as shown in the following table:

Current altimeter setting	Lowest usable flight level
29.92 (or higher)	180
29.91 through 29.42	185
29.41 through 28.92	190
28.91 through 28.42	195
28.41 through 27.92	200
27.91 through 27.42	205
27.41 through 26.92	210

c) To convert minimum altitude prescribed under §§ 91.119 and 91.177 to the minimum flight level, the pilot shall take the flight level equivalent of the minimum altitude in feet and add the appropriate number of feet specified below, according to the current reported altimeter setting:

Current altimeter setting	Adjustment factor
29.92 (or higher)	None
29.91 through 29.42	500
29.41 through 28.92	1,000
28.91 through 28.42	1,500
28.41 through 27.92	2,000
27.91 through 27.42	2,500
27.41 through 26.92	3,000

§ 91.123 Compliance with ATC clearances and instructions.

a) When an ATC clearance has been obtained, no pilot in command may deviate from that clearance unless an amended clearance is obtained, an emergency exists, or the deviation is in response to a traffic alert and collision avoidance system resolution advisory. However, except in Class A airspace, a pilot may cancel an IFR flight plan if the operation is being conducted in VFR weather conditions. When a pilot is uncertain of an ATC clearance, that pilot shall immediately request clarification from ATC.

b) Except in an emergency, no person may operate an aircraft contrary to an ATC instruction in an area in which air traffic control is exercised.

c) Each pilot in command who, in an emergency, or in response to a traffic alert and collision avoidance system resolution advisory, deviates from an ATC clearance or instruction shall notify ATC of that deviation as soon as possible.

d) Each pilot in command who (though not deviating from a rule of this subpart) is given priority by ATC in an emergency, shall submit a detailed report of that emergency within 48 hours to the manager of that ATC facility, if requested by ATC.

e) Unless otherwise authorized by ATC, no person operating an aircraft may operate that aircraft according to any clearance or instruction that has been issued to the pilot of another aircraft for radar air traffic control purposes.

§ 91.125 ATC light signals.

ATC light signals have the meaning shown in the following table:

Color and type of signal	Meaning with respect to aircraft on the surface	Meaning with respect to aircraft in flight
Steady green	Cleared for takeoff	Cleared to land.
Flashing green	Cleared to taxi	Return for landing (to be followed by steady green at proper time).
Steady red	Stop	Give way to other aircraft and continue circling.
Flashing red	Taxi clear of runway in use	Airport unsafe–do not land.
Flashing white	Return to starting point on airport	Not applicable.
Alternating red and green	Exercise extreme caution	Exercise extreme caution.

§ 91.147 Passenger carrying flights for compensation or hire.

Each Operator conducting passenger-carrying flights for compensation or hire must meet the following requirements unless all flights are conducted under § 91.146.

a) For the purposes of this section and for drug and alcohol testing, **Operator** means any person conducting nonstop passenger-carrying flights in an airplane or helicopter for compensation or hire in accordance with §§ 119.1(e)(2), 135.1(a)(5), or 121.1(d), of this chapter that begin and end at the same airport and are conducted within a 25-statute mile radius of that airport.

b) An Operator must comply with the safety provisions of part 136, subpart A of this chapter, and apply for and receive a Letter of Authorization from the responsible Flight Standards office.

c) Each application for a Letter of Authorization must include the following information:

1) Name of Operator, agent, and any d/b/a (doing-business-as) under which that Operator does business;

2) Principal business address and mailing address;

3) Principal place of business (if different from business address);

4) Name of person responsible for management of the business;

5) Name of person responsible for aircraft maintenance;

6) Type of aircraft, registration number(s), and make/model/series; and

7) An Antidrug and Alcohol Misuse Prevention Program registration.

d) The Operator must register and implement its drug and alcohol testing programs in accordance with part 120 of this chapter.

e) The Operator must comply with the provisions of the Letter of Authorization received.

§ 91.151 Fuel requirements for flight in VFR conditions.

a) No person may begin a flight in an airplane under VFR conditions unless (considering wind and forecast weather conditions) there is enough fuel to fly to the first point of intended landing and, assuming normal cruising speed–

1) During the day, to fly after that for at least 30 minutes; or

2) At night, to fly after that for at least 45 minutes.

b) *Rotorcraft.*

§ 91.155 Basic VFR weather minimums.

a) Except as provided in paragraph (b) of this section and § 91.157, no person may operate an aircraft under VFR when the flight visibility is less, or at a distance from clouds that is less, than that prescribed for the corresponding altitude and class of airspace in the following table:

(the following table is abbreviated for formatting and ease of reading)

Airspace	Flight visibility	Cloud Clearance
Class A	*n/a*	*n/a*
Class B	*3 sm*	*Clear*
Class C	*3 sm*	*500/1,000/2,000*
Class D	*3 sm*	*500/1,000/2,000*
Class E:		
Less than 10,000 ft MSL	*3 sm*	*500/1,000/2,000*
At or above 10,000 ft MSL	*5 sm*	*1,000/1,000/1*
Class G:		
1,200 ft or less AGL (regardless of MSL)		
Day, except as provided in 91.155(b)	*1 sm*	*Clear*
Night, except as provided in 91.155(b)	*3 sm*	*500/1,000/2,000*
More than 1,200 ft AGL but less than 10,000 ft MSL		
Day	*1 sm*	*500/1,000/2,000*
Night	*3 sm*	*500/1,000/2,000*
More than 1,200 ft AGL and at or above 10,000 ft MSL	*5 sm*	*1,000/1,000/1*

b) **Class G Airspace**. Notwithstanding the provisions of paragraph (a) of this section, the following operations may be conducted in Class G airspace below 1,200 feet above the surface:

1) *Helicopter*.

2) **Airplane, powered parachute, or weight-shift-control aircraft**. If the visibility is less than 3 statute miles but not less than 1 statute mile

during night hours and you are operating in an airport traffic pattern within 1⁄2 mile of the runway, you may operate an airplane, powered parachute, or weight-shift-control aircraft clear of clouds.

c) Except as provided in § 91.157, no person may operate an aircraft beneath the ceiling under VFR within the lateral boundaries of controlled airspace designated to the surface for an airport when the ceiling is less than 1,000 feet.

d) Except as provided in § 91.157 of this part, no person may take off or land an aircraft, or enter the traffic pattern of an airport, under VFR, within the lateral boundaries of the surface areas of Class B, Class C, Class D, or Class E airspace designated for an airport–

1) Unless ground visibility at that airport is at least 3 statute miles; or

2) If ground visibility is not reported at that airport, unless flight visibility during landing or takeoff, or while operating in the traffic pattern is at least 3 statute miles.

e) For the purpose of this section, an aircraft operating at the base altitude of a Class E airspace area is considered to be within the airspace directly below that area.

§ 91.157 Special VFR weather minimums.

a) Except as provided in appendix D, section 3, of this part, special VFR operations may be conducted under the weather minimums and requirements of this section, instead of those contained in § 91.155, below 10,000 feet MSL within the airspace contained by the upward extension of the lateral boundaries of the controlled airspace designated to the surface for an airport.

b) Special VFR operations may only be conducted–

1) With an ATC clearance;

2) Clear of clouds;

3) Except for helicopters, when flight visibility is at least 1 statute mile; and

4) Except for helicopters, between sunrise and sunset (or in Alaska, when the sun is 6 degrees or more below the horizon) unless–

i) The person being granted the ATC clearance meets the applicable requirements for instrument flight under part 61 of this chapter; and

ii) The aircraft is equipped as required in § 91.205(d).

c) No person may take off or land an aircraft (other than a helicopter) under special VFR–

1) Unless ground visibility is at least 1 statute mile; or

2) If ground visibility is not reported, unless flight visibility is at least 1 statute mile. For the purposes of this paragraph, the term flight visibility includes the visibility from the cockpit of an aircraft in takeoff position if:

i) The flight is conducted under this part 91; and

ii) The airport at which the aircraft is located is a satellite airport that does not have weather reporting capabilities.

d) The determination of visibility by a pilot in accordance with paragraph (c)(2) of this section is not an official weather report or an official ground visibility report.

§ 91.159 VFR cruising altitude or flight level.

Except while holding in a holding pattern of 2 minutes or less, or while turning, each person operating an aircraft under VFR in level cruising flight more than 3,000 feet above the surface shall maintain the appropriate altitude or flight level prescribed below, unless otherwise authorized by ATC:

a) When operating below 18,000 feet MSL and–

1) On a magnetic course of zero degrees through 179 degrees, any odd thousand foot MSL altitude + 500 feet (such as 3,500, 5,500, or 7,500); or

2) On a magnetic course of 180 degrees through 359 degrees, any even thousand foot MSL altitude + 500 feet (such as 4,500, 6,500, or 8,500).

b) When operating above 18,000 feet MSL, maintain the altitude or flight level assigned by ATC.

§ 91.203 Civil aircraft: Certifications required.

a) Except as provided in § 91.715, no person may operate a civil aircraft unless it has within it the following:

1) An appropriate and current airworthiness certificate. Each U.S. airworthiness certificate used to comply with this subparagraph (except a special flight permit, a copy of the applicable operations specifications issued under § 21.197(c) of this chapter, appropriate sections of the air carrier manual required by parts 121 and 135 of this chapter containing that portion of the operations specifications issued under § 21.197(c), or an authorization under § 91.611) must have on it the registration number assigned to the aircraft under part 47 of this chapter. However, the airworthiness certificate need not have on it an assigned special identification number before 10 days after that number is first affixed to the aircraft. A revised airworthiness certificate having on it an assigned special identification number, that has been affixed to an aircraft, may only be obtained upon application to the responsible Flight Standards office.

2) An effective U.S. registration certificate issued to its owner or, for operation within the United States, the second copy of the Aircraft registration Application as provided for in § 47.31(c), a Certificate of Aircraft registration as provided in part 48, or a registration certification issued under the laws of a foreign country.

b) No person may operate a civil aircraft unless the airworthiness certificate required by paragraph (a) of this section or a special flight authorization issued under § 91.715 is displayed at the cabin or cockpit entrance so that it is legible to passengers or crew.

c) No person may operate an aircraft with a fuel tank installed within the passenger compartment or a baggage compartment unless the installation was accomplished pursuant to part 43 of this chapter, and a copy of FAA Form 337 authorizing that installation is on board the aircraft.

d) No person may operate a civil airplane (domestic or foreign) into or out of an airport in the United States unless it complies with the fuel venting and exhaust emissions requirements of part 34 of this chapter.

§ 91.205 Powered civil aircraft with standard category U.S. airworthiness certificates: Instrument and equipment requirements.

a) **General**. Except as provided in paragraphs (c)(3) and (e) of this section, no person may operate a powered civil aircraft with a standard category U.S. airworthiness certificate in any operation described in paragraphs (b) through (f) of this section unless that aircraft contains the instruments and equipment specified in those paragraphs (or FAA-approved equivalents) for that type of operation, and those instruments and items of equipment are in operable condition.

b) **Visual-flight rules (day)**. For VFR flight during the day, the following instruments and equipment are required:

1) Airspeed indicator.

2) Altimeter.

3) Magnetic direction indicator.

4) Tachometer for each engine.

5) Oil pressure gauge for each engine using pressure system.

6) Temperature gauge for each liquid-cooled engine.

7) Oil temperature gauge for each air-cooled engine.

8) Manifold pressure gauge for each altitude engine.

9) Fuel gauge indicating the quantity of fuel in each tank.

10) Landing gear position indicator, if the aircraft has a retractable landing gear.

11) For small civil airplanes certificated after March 11, 1996, in accordance with part 23 of this chapter, an approved aviation red or aviation white anticollision light system. In the event of failure of any light of the anticollision light system, operation of the aircraft may continue to a location where repairs or replacement can be made.

12) If the aircraft is operated for hire over water and beyond power-off gliding distance from shore, approved flotation gear readily available to each occupant and, unless the aircraft is operating under part 121 of this subchapter, at least one pyrotechnic signaling device. As used in this section, "shore" means that area of the land adjacent to the water which is above the high water mark and excludes land areas which are intermittently under water.

13) An approved safety belt with an approved metal-to-metal latching device, or other approved restraint system for each occupant 2 years of age or older.

14) For small civil airplanes manufactured after July 18, 1978, an approved shoulder harness or restraint system for each front seat. For small civil airplanes manufactured after December 12, 1986, an approved shoulder harness or restraint system for all seats. Shoulder harnesses installed at flightcrew stations must permit the flightcrew member, when seated and with the safety belt and shoulder harness fastened, to perform all functions necessary for flight operations. For purposes of this paragraph–

i) The date of manufacture of an airplane is the date the inspection acceptance records reflect that the airplane is complete and meets the FAA-approved type design data; and

ii) A front seat is a seat located at a flightcrew member station or any seat located alongside such a seat.

15) An emergency locator transmitter, if required by § 91.207.

16) *Reserved*.

17) *Rotorcraft.*

c) **Visual flight rules (night).** For VFR flight at night, the following instruments and equipment are required:

1) Instruments and equipment specified in paragraph (b) of this section.

2) Approved position lights.

3) An approved aviation red or aviation white anticollision light system on all U.S.-registered civil aircraft. Anticollision light systems initially installed after August 11, 1971, on aircraft for which a type certificate was issued or applied for before August 11, 1971, must at least meet the anticollision light standards of part 23, 25, 27, or 29 of this chapter, as applicable, that were in effect on August 10, 1971, except that the color may be either aviation red or aviation white. In the event of failure of any light of the anticollision light system, operations with the aircraft may be continued to a stop where repairs or replacement can be made.

4) If the aircraft is operated for hire, one electric landing light.

5) An adequate source of electrical energy for all installed electrical and radio equipment.

6) One spare set of fuses, or three spare fuses of each kind required, that are accessible to the pilot in flight.

d) **Instrument flight rules**. For IFR flight, the following instruments and equipment are required:

1) Instruments and equipment specified in paragraph (b) of this section, and, for night flight, instruments and equipment specified in paragraph (c) of this section.

2) Two-way radio communication and navigation equipment suitable for the route to be flown.

3) Gyroscopic rate-of-turn indicator, except on the following aircraft:

i) Airplanes with a third attitude instrument system usable through flight attitudes of 360 degrees of pitch and roll and installed in accordance with the instrument requirements prescribed in § 121.305(j) of this chapter; and

ii) *Rotorcraft.*

4) Slip-skid indicator.

5) Sensitive altimeter adjustable for barometric pressure.

6) A clock displaying hours, minutes, and seconds with a sweep-second pointer or digital presentation.

7) Generator or alternator of adequate capacity.

8) Gyroscopic pitch and bank indicator (artificial horizon).

9) Gyroscopic direction indicator (directional gyro or equivalent).

e) **Flight at and above 24,000 feet MSL (FL 240)**. If VOR navigation equipment is required under paragraph (d)(2) of this section, no person may operate a U.S.-registered civil aircraft within the 50 states and the District of Columbia at or above FL 240 unless that aircraft is equipped with approved DME or a suitable RNAV system. When the DME or RNAV system required by this paragraph fails at and above FL 240, the pilot in command of the aircraft must notify ATC immediately, and then may continue operations at and above FL 240 to the next airport of intended landing where repairs or replacement of the equipment can be made.

f) *Category II operations.*

g) *Category III operations.*

h) *Night vision goggle operations.*

i) *Part 121 and 135 exclusions.*

§ 91.207 Emergency locator transmitters.

a) Except as provided in paragraphs (e) and (f) of this section, no person may operate a U.S.-registered civil airplane unless–

1) *Certain Part 121, 125, and 135 operations*; or

2) For operations other than those specified in paragraph (a)(1) of this section, there must be attached to the airplane an approved personal type or an approved automatic type emergency locator transmitter that is in operable condition, except that after June 21, 1995, an emergency locator transmitter that meets the requirements of TSO-C91 may not be used for new installations.

b) Each emergency locator transmitter required by paragraph (a) of this section must be attached to the airplane in such a manner that the probability of damage to the transmitter in the event of crash impact is minimized. Fixed and deployable automatic type transmitters must be attached to the airplane as far aft as practicable.

c) Batteries used in the emergency locator transmitters required by paragraphs (a) and (b) of this section must be replaced (or recharged, if the batteries are rechargeable)–

1) When the transmitter has been in use for more than 1 cumulative hour; or

2) When 50 percent of their useful life (or, for rechargeable batteries, 50 percent of their useful life of charge) has expired, as established by the transmitter manufacturer under its approval.

The new expiration date for replacing (or recharging) the battery must be legibly marked on the outside of the transmitter and entered in the aircraft maintenance record. Paragraph (c)(2) of this section does not apply to batteries (such as water-activated batteries) that are essentially unaffected during probable storage intervals.

d) Each emergency locator transmitter required by paragraph (a) of this section must be inspected within 12 calendar months after the last inspection for–

1) Proper installation;

2) Battery corrosion;

3) Operation of the controls and crash sensor; and

4) The presence of a sufficient signal radiated from its antenna.

e) Notwithstanding paragraph (a) of this section, a person may–

1) Ferry a newly acquired airplane from the place where possession of it was taken to a place where the emergency locator transmitter is to be installed; and

2) Ferry an airplane with an inoperative emergency locator transmitter from a place where repairs or replacements cannot be made to a place where they can be made.

No person other than required crewmembers may be carried aboard an airplane being ferried under paragraph (e) of this section.

f) Paragraph (a) of this section does not apply to–

1) Before January 1, 2004, turbojet-powered aircraft;

2) *Scheduled air carrier flights*;

3) Aircraft while engaged in training operations conducted entirely within a 50-nautical mile radius of the airport from which such local flight operations began;

4) Aircraft while engaged in flight operations incident to design and testing;

5) New aircraft while engaged in flight operations incident to their manufacture, preparation, and delivery;

6) Aircraft while engaged in flight operations incident to the aerial application of chemicals and other substances for agricultural purposes;

7) Aircraft certificated by the Administrator for research and development purposes;

8) Aircraft while used for showing compliance with regulations, crew training, exhibition, air racing, or market surveys;

9) Aircraft equipped to carry not more than one person.

10) An aircraft during any period for which the transmitter has been temporarily removed for inspection, repair, modification, or replacement, subject to the following:

i) No person may operate the aircraft unless the aircraft records contain an entry which includes the date of initial removal, the make, model, serial number, and reason for removing the transmitter, and a placard located in view of the pilot to show "ELT not installed."

ii) No person may operate the aircraft more than 90 days after the ELT is initially removed from the aircraft; and

11) On and after January 1, 2004, aircraft with a maximum payload capacity of more than 18,000 pounds when used in air transportation.

§ 91.209 Aircraft lights.

No person may:

a) During the period from sunset to sunrise (or, in Alaska, during the period a prominent unlighted object cannot be seen from a distance of 3 statute miles or the sun is more than 6 degrees below the horizon)–

1) Operate an aircraft unless it has lighted position lights;

2) Park or move an aircraft in, or in dangerous proximity to, a night flight operations area of an airport unless the aircraft–

i) Is clearly illuminated;

ii) Has lighted position lights; or

iii) is in an area that is marked by obstruction lights;

3) Anchor an aircraft unless the aircraft–

i) Has lighted anchor lights; or

ii) Is in an area where anchor lights are not required on vessels; or

b) Operate an aircraft that is equipped with an anticollision light system, unless it has lighted anticollision lights. However, the anticollision lights need not be lighted when the pilot-in-command determines that, because of operating conditions, it would be in the interest of safety to turn the lights off.

§ 91.211 Supplemental oxygen.

a) **General**. No person may operate a civil aircraft of U.S. registry–

1) At cabin pressure altitudes above 12,500 feet (MSL) up to and including 14,000 feet (MSL) unless the required minimum flight crew is provided with and uses supplemental oxygen for that part of the flight at those altitudes that is of more than 30 minutes duration;

2) At cabin pressure altitudes above 14,000 feet (MSL) unless the required minimum flight crew is provided with and uses supplemental oxygen during the entire flight time at those altitudes; and

3) At cabin pressure altitudes above 15,000 feet (MSL) unless each occupant of the aircraft is provided with supplemental oxygen.

b) **Pressurized cabin aircraft**.

1) No person may operate a civil aircraft of U.S. registry with a pressurized cabin–

i) At flight altitudes above flight level 250 unless at least a 10-minute supply of supplemental oxygen, in addition to any oxygen required to satisfy paragraph (a) of this section, is available for each occupant of the aircraft for use in the event that a descent is necessitated by loss of cabin pressurization; and

ii) At flight altitudes above flight level 350 unless one pilot at the controls of the airplane is wearing and using an oxygen mask that is secured and sealed and that either supplies oxygen at all times or automatically supplies oxygen whenever the cabin pressure altitude of the airplane exceeds 14,000 feet (MSL), except that the one pilot need not wear and use an oxygen mask while at or below flight level 410 if there are two pilots at the controls and each pilot has a quick-donning type of oxygen mask that can be placed on the face with one hand from the ready position within 5 seconds, supplying oxygen and properly secured and sealed.

2) Notwithstanding paragraph (b)(1)(ii) of this section, if for any reason at any time it is necessary for one pilot to leave the controls of the aircraft when operating at flight altitudes above flight level 350, the remaining pilot at the controls shall put on and use an oxygen mask until the other pilot has returned to that crewmember's station.

§ 91.213 Inoperative instruments and equipment.

a) Except as provided in paragraph (d) of this section, no person may take off an aircraft with inoperative instruments or equipment installed unless the following conditions are met:

1) An approved Minimum Equipment List exists for that aircraft.

2) The aircraft has within it a letter of authorization, issued by the responsible Flight Standards office, authorizing operation of the aircraft under the Minimum Equipment List. The letter of authorization may be obtained by written request of the airworthiness certificate holder. The Minimum Equipment List and the letter of authorization constitute a supplemental type certificate for the aircraft.

3) The approved Minimum Equipment List must–

i) Be prepared in accordance with the limitations specified in paragraph (b) of this section; and

ii) Provide for the operation of the aircraft with the instruments and equipment in an inoperable condition.

4) The aircraft records available to the pilot must include an entry describing the inoperable instruments and equipment.

5) The aircraft is operated under all applicable conditions and limitations contained in the Minimum Equipment List and the letter authorizing the use of the list.

b) The following instruments and equipment may not be included in a Minimum Equipment List:

1) Instruments and equipment that are either specifically or otherwise required by the airworthiness requirements under which the aircraft is type certificated and which are essential for safe operations under all operating conditions.

2) Instruments and equipment required by an airworthiness directive to be in operable condition unless the airworthiness directive provides otherwise.

3) Instruments and equipment required for specific operations by this part.

c) A person authorized to use an approved Minimum Equipment List issued for a specific aircraft under subpart K of this part, part 121, 125, or 135 of this chapter must use that Minimum Equipment List to comply with the requirements in this section.

d) Except for operations conducted in accordance with paragraph (a) or (c) of this section, a person may takeoff an aircraft in operations conducted under this part with inoperative instruments and equipment without an approved Minimum Equipment List provided–

1) The flight operation is conducted in a–

i) Rotorcraft, non-turbine-powered airplane, glider, lighter-than-air aircraft, powered parachute, or weight-shift-control aircraft, for which a master minimum equipment list has not been developed; or

ii) Small rotorcraft, nonturbine-powered small airplane, glider, or lighter-than-air aircraft for which a Master Minimum Equipment List has been developed; and

2) The inoperative instruments and equipment are not–

i) Part of the VFR-day type certification instruments and equipment prescribed in the applicable airworthiness regulations under which the aircraft was type certificated;

ii) Indicated as required on the aircraft's equipment list, or on the Kinds of Operations Equipment List for the kind of flight operation being conducted;

iii) Required by § 91.205 or any other rule of this part for the specific kind of flight operation being conducted; or

iv) Required to be operational by an airworthiness directive; and

3) The inoperative instruments and equipment are–

i) Removed from the aircraft, the cockpit control placarded, and the maintenance recorded in accordance with § 43.9 of this chapter; or

ii) Deactivated and placarded "Inoperative." If deactivation of the inoperative instrument or equipment involves maintenance, it must be accomplished and recorded in accordance with part 43 of this chapter; and

4) A determination is made by a pilot, who is certificated and appropriately rated under part 61 of this chapter, or by a person, who is certificated and appropriately rated to perform maintenance on the aircraft, that the inoperative instrument or equipment does not constitute a hazard to the aircraft.

An aircraft with inoperative instruments or equipment as provided in paragraph (d) of this section is considered to be in a properly altered condition acceptable to the Administrator.

e) Notwithstanding any other provision of this section, an aircraft with inoperable instruments or equipment may be operated under a special flight permit issued in accordance with §§ 21.197 and 21.199 of this chapter.

§ 91.215 ATC transponder and altitude reporting equipment and use.

a) **All airspace: U.S.-registered civil aircraft**. For operations not conducted under part 121 or 135 of this chapter, ATC transponder equipment installed must meet the performance and environmental requirements of any class of TSO-C74b (Mode A) or any class of TSO-C74c (Mode A with altitude reporting capability) as appropriate, or the appropriate class of TSO-C112 (Mode S).

b) **All airspace**. Unless otherwise authorized or directed by ATC, and except as provided in paragraph (e)(1) of this section, no person may operate an aircraft in the airspace described in paragraphs (b)(1) through (5) of this section, unless that aircraft is equipped with an operable coded radar beacon transponder having either Mode 3/A 4096 code capability, replying to Mode 3/A interrogations with the code specified by ATC, or a Mode S capability, replying to Mode 3/A interrogations with the code specified by ATC and intermode and Mode S interrogations in accordance with the applicable provisions specified in TSO C-112, and that aircraft is equipped with automatic pressure altitude reporting equipment having a Mode C capability that automatically replies to Mode C interrogations by transmitting pressure altitude information in 100-foot increments. The requirements of this paragraph (b) apply to–

1) **All aircraft**. In Class A, Class B, and Class C airspace areas;

2) **All aircraft**. In all airspace within 30 nautical miles of an airport listed in appendix D, section 1 of this part from the surface upward to 10,000 feet MSL;

3) Notwithstanding paragraph (b)(2) of this section, any aircraft which was not originally certificated with an engine-driven electrical system or which has not subsequently been certified with such a system installed, balloon or glider may conduct operations in the airspace within 30 nautical miles of an airport listed in appendix D, section 1 of this part provided such operations are conducted–

i) Outside any Class A, Class B, or Class C airspace area; and

ii) Below the altitude of the ceiling of a Class B or Class C airspace area designated for an airport or 10,000 feet MSL, whichever is lower; and

4) All aircraft in all airspace above the ceiling and within the lateral boundaries of a Class B or Class C airspace area designated for an airport upward to 10,000 feet MSL; and

5) All aircraft except any aircraft which was not originally certificated with an engine-driven electrical system or which has not subsequently been certified with such a system installed, balloon, or glider–

i) In all airspace of the 48 contiguous states and the District of Columbia at and above 10,000 feet MSL, excluding the airspace at and below 2,500 feet above the surface; and

ii) In the airspace from the surface to 10,000 feet MSL within a 10-nautical-mile radius of any airport listed in appendix D, section 2 of this part, excluding the airspace below 1,200 feet outside of the lateral boundaries of the surface area of the airspace designated for that airport.

c) **Transponder-on operation**. Except as provided in paragraph (e)(2) of this section, while in the airspace as specified in paragraph (b) of this section or in all controlled airspace, each person operating an aircraft equipped with an operable ATC transponder maintained in accordance with § 91.413 shall operate the transponder, including Mode C equipment if installed, and shall reply on the appropriate code or as assigned by ATC, unless otherwise directed by ATC when transmitting would jeopardize the safe execution of air traffic control functions.

d) **ATC authorized deviations**. Requests for ATC authorized deviations must be made to the ATC facility having jurisdiction over the concerned airspace within the time periods specified as follows:

1) For operation of an aircraft with an operating transponder but without operating automatic pressure altitude reporting equipment having a Mode C capability, the request may be made at any time.

2) For operation of an aircraft with an inoperative transponder to the airport of ultimate destination, including any intermediate stops, or to proceed to a place where suitable repairs can be made or both, the request may be made at any time.

3) For operation of an aircraft that is not equipped with a transponder, the request must be made at least one hour before the proposed operation.

e) *Unmanned aircraft.*

§ 91.225 Automatic Dependent Surveillance-Broadcast (ADS-B) Out equipment and use.

a) After January 1, 2020, unless otherwise authorized by ATC, no person may operate an aircraft in Class A airspace unless the aircraft has equipment installed that–

1) Meets the performance requirements in TSO-C166b, Extended Squitter Automatic Dependent Surveillance-Broadcast (ADS-B) and Traffic Information Service-Broadcast (TIS-B) Equipment Operating on the Radio Frequency of 1090 Megahertz (MHz); and

2) Meets the requirements of § 91.227.

b) After January 1, 2020, except as prohibited in paragraph (i)(2) of this section or unless otherwise authorized by ATC, no person may operate an aircraft below 18,000 feet MSL and in airspace described in paragraph (d) of this section unless the aircraft has equipment installed that–

1) Meets the performance requirements in–

i) TSO-C166b; or

ii) TSO-C154c, Universal Access Transceiver (UAT) Automatic Dependent Surveillance-Broadcast (ADS-B) Equipment Operating on the Frequency of 978 MHz;

2) Meets the requirements of § 91.227.

c) Operators with equipment installed with an approved deviation under § 21.618 of this chapter also are in compliance with this section.

d) After January 1, 2020, except as prohibited in paragraph (i)(2) of this section or unless otherwise authorized by ATC, no person may operate an aircraft in the following airspace unless the aircraft has equipment installed that meets the requirements in paragraph (b) of this section:

1) Class B and Class C airspace areas;

2) Except as provided for in paragraph (e) of this section, within 30 nautical miles of an airport listed in appendix D, section 1 to this part from the surface upward to 10,000 feet MSL;

3) Above the ceiling and within the lateral boundaries of a Class B or Class C airspace area designated for an airport upward to 10,000 feet MSL;

4) Except as provided in paragraph (e) of this section, Class E airspace within the 48 contiguous states and the District of Columbia at and above 10,000 feet MSL, excluding the airspace at and below 2,500 feet above the surface; and

5) Class E airspace at and above 3,000 feet MSL over the Gulf of Mexico from the coastline of the United States out to 12 nautical miles.

e) The requirements of paragraph (b) of this section do not apply to any aircraft that was not originally certificated with an electrical system, or that has not subsequently been certified with such a system installed, including balloons and gliders. These aircraft may conduct operations without ADS-B Out in the airspace specified in paragraphs (d)(2) and (d)(4) of this section. Operations authorized by this section must be conducted–

1) Outside any Class B or Class C airspace area; and

2) Below the altitude of the ceiling of a Class B or Class C airspace area designated for an airport, or 10,000 feet MSL, whichever is lower.

f) Except as prohibited in paragraph (i)(2) of this section, each person operating an aircraft equipped with ADS-B Out must operate this equipment in the transmit mode at all times unless–

1) Otherwise authorized by the FAA when the aircraft is performing a sensitive government mission for national defense, homeland security, intelligence or law enforcement purposes and transmitting would compromise the operations security of the mission or pose a safety risk to the aircraft, crew, or people and property in the air or on the ground; or

2) Otherwise directed by ATC when transmitting would jeopardize the safe execution of air traffic control functions.

g) Requests for ATC authorized deviations from the requirements of this section must be made to the ATC facility having jurisdiction over the concerned airspace within the time periods specified as follows:

1) For operation of an aircraft with an inoperative ADS-B Out, to the airport of ultimate destination, including any intermediate stops, or to proceed to a place where suitable repairs can be made or both, the request may be made at any time.

2) For operation of an aircraft that is not equipped with ADS-B Out, the request must be made at least 1 hour before the proposed operation.

h) The standards required in this section are incorporated by reference with the approval of the Director of the Office of the Federal Register under 5 U.S.C. 552(a) and 1 CFR part 51. All approved materials are available for inspection at the FAA's Office of Rulemaking (ARM-1), 800 Independence Avenue, SW., Washington, DC 20590 (telephone 202-267-9677), or at the National Archives and Records Administration (NARA). For information on the availability of this material at NARA, call 202-741-6030, or go to http://www.archives.gov/federal_register/code_of_federal_regulations/ibr_locations.html. This material is also available from the sources indicated in paragraphs (h)(1) and (h)(2) of this section.

1) Copies of Technical Standard Order (TSO)-C166b, Extended Squitter Automatic Dependent Surveillance-Broadcast (ADS-B) and Traffic Information Service-Broadcast (TIS-B) Equipment Operating on the Radio Frequency of 1090 Megahertz (MHz) (December 2, 2009) and TSO-C154c, Universal Access Transceiver (UAT) Automatic Dependent Surveillance-Broadcast (ADS-B) Equipment Operating on the Frequency of 978 MHz (December 2, 2009) may be obtained from the U.S. Department of Transportation, Subsequent Distribution Office, DOT Warehouse M30, Ardmore East Business Center, 3341 Q 75th Avenue, Landover, MD 20785; telephone (301) 322-5377. Copies of TSO -C166B and TSO-C154c are also available on the FAA's Web site, at http://www.faa.gov/aircraft/air_cert/design_approvals/tso/. Select the link "Search Technical Standard Orders."

2) Copies of Section 2, Equipment Performance Requirements and Test Procedures, of RTCA DO-260B, Minimum Operational Performance Standards for 1090 MHz Extended Squitter Automatic Dependent Surveillance-Broadcast (ADS-B) and Traffic Information Services-Broadcast (TIS-B), December 2, 2009 (referenced in TSO-C166b) and Section 2, Equipment Performance Requirements and Test Procedures, of RTCA DO-282B, Minimum Operational Performance Standards for Universal Access Transceiver (UAT) Automatic Dependent Surveillance-Broadcast (ADS-B), December 2, 2009 (referenced in TSO C-154c) may be obtained from RTCA, Inc., 1828 L Street, NW., Suite 805, Washington, DC 20036-5133, telephone 202-833-9339. Copies of RTCA DO-260B and RTCA DO-282B are also available on RTCA Inc.'s Web site, at http://www.rtca.org/onlinecart/allproducts.cfm.

i) *Unmanned aircraft.*

§ 91.407 Operation after maintenance, preventive maintenance, rebuilding, or alteration.

a) No person may operate any aircraft that has undergone maintenance, preventive maintenance, rebuilding, or alteration unless–

1) It has been approved for return to service by a person authorized under § 43.7 of this chapter; and

2) The maintenance record entry required by § 43.9 or § 43.11, as applicable, of this chapter has been made.

b) No person may carry any person (other than crewmembers) in an aircraft that has been maintained, rebuilt, or altered in a manner that may have appreciably changed its flight characteristics or substantially affected its operation in flight until an appropriately rated pilot with at least a private pilot certificate flies the aircraft, makes an operational check of the maintenance performed or alteration made, and logs the flight in the aircraft records.

c) The aircraft does not have to be flown as required by paragraph (b) of this section if, prior to flight, ground tests, inspection, or both show conclusively that the maintenance, preventive maintenance, rebuilding, or alteration has not appreciably changed the flight characteristics or substantially affected the flight operation of the aircraft.

§ 91.409 Inspections.

a) Except as provided in paragraph (c) of this section, no person may operate an aircraft unless, within the preceding 12 calendar months, it has had–

1) An annual inspection in accordance with part 43 of this chapter and has been approved for return to service by a person authorized by § 43.7 of this chapter; or

2) An inspection for the issuance of an airworthiness certificate in accordance with part 21 of this chapter.

No inspection performed under paragraph (b) of this section may be substituted for any inspection required by this paragraph unless it is performed by a person authorized to perform annual inspections and is entered as an "annual" inspection in the required maintenance records.

b) Except as provided in paragraph (c) of this section, no person may operate an aircraft carrying any person (other than a crewmember) for hire, and no person may give flight instruction for hire in an aircraft which that person provides, unless within the preceding 100 hours of time in service the aircraft has received an annual or 100-hour inspection and been approved for return to service in accordance with part 43 of this chapter or has received an inspection for the issuance of an airworthiness certificate in accordance with part 21 of this chapter. The 100-hour limitation may be exceeded by not more than 10 hours while en route to reach a place where the inspection can be done. The excess time used to reach a place where the inspection can be done must be included in computing the next 100 hours of time in service.

c) Paragraphs (a) and (b) of this section do not apply to–

1) An aircraft that carries a special flight permit, a current experimental certificate, or a light-sport or provisional airworthiness certificate;

2) *Certain Part 125 and 135 operations;*

3) An aircraft subject to the requirements of paragraph (d) or (e) of this section; or

4) *Certain turbine-powered rotorcraft operations.*

d) **Progressive inspection**. Each registered owner or operator of an aircraft desiring to use a progressive inspection program must submit a written request to the responsible Flight Standards office, and shall provide–

1) A certificated mechanic holding an inspection authorization, a certificated airframe repair station, or the manufacturer of the aircraft to supervise or conduct the progressive inspection;

2) A current inspection procedures manual available and readily understandable to pilot and maintenance personnel containing, in detail–

i) An explanation of the progressive inspection, including the continuity of inspection responsibility, the making of reports, and the keeping of records and technical reference material;

ii) An inspection schedule, specifying the intervals in hours or days when routine and detailed inspections will be performed and including instructions for exceeding an inspection interval by not more than 10 hours while en route and for changing an inspection interval because of service experience;

iii) Sample routine and detailed inspection forms and instructions for their use; and

iv) Sample reports and records and instructions for their use;

3) Enough housing and equipment for necessary disassembly and proper inspection of the aircraft; and

4) Appropriate current technical information for the aircraft.

The frequency and detail of the progressive inspection shall provide for the complete inspection of the aircraft within each 12 calendar months and be consistent with the manufacturer's recommendations, field service experience, and the kind of operation in which the aircraft is engaged. The progressive inspection schedule must ensure that the aircraft, at all times, will be airworthy and will conform to all applicable FAA aircraft specifications, type certificate data sheets, airworthiness directives, and other approved data. If the progressive inspection is discontinued, the owner or operator shall immediately notify the responsible Flight Standards office, in writing, of the discontinuance. After the discontinuance, the first annual inspection under § 91.409(a)(1) is due within 12 calendar months after the last complete inspection of the aircraft under the progressive inspection. The 100-hour inspection under § 91.409(b) is due within 100 hours after that complete inspection. A complete inspection of the aircraft, for the purpose of determining when the annual and 100-hour inspections are due, requires a detailed inspection of the aircraft and all its components in accordance with the progressive inspection. A routine inspection of the aircraft and a detailed inspection of several components is not considered to be a complete inspection.

e) *Large airplanes (to which part 125 is not applicable), turbojet multiengine airplanes, turbopropeller-powered multiengine airplanes, and turbine-powered rotorcraft.*

f) *Selection of inspection program under paragraph (e) of this section.*

g) *Inspection program approved under paragraph (e) of this section.*

h) *Certain changes from one inspection program to another.*

§ 91.411 Altimeter system and altitude reporting equipment tests and inspections.

a) No person may operate an airplane, or helicopter, in controlled airspace under IFR unless–

1) Within the preceding 24 calendar months, each static pressure system, each altimeter instrument, and each automatic pressure altitude reporting system has been tested and inspected and found to comply with appendices E and F of part 43 of this chapter;

2) Except for the use of system drain and alternate static pressure valves, following any opening and closing of the static pressure system, that system has been tested and inspected and found to comply with paragraph (a), appendix E, of part 43 of this chapter; and

3) Following installation or maintenance on the automatic pressure altitude reporting system of the ATC transponder where data correspondence error could be introduced, the integrated system has been tested, inspected, and found to comply with paragraph (c), appendix E, of part 43 of this chapter.

b) The tests required by paragraph (a) of this section must be conducted by–

1) The manufacturer of the airplane, or helicopter, on which the tests and inspections are to be performed;

2) A certificated repair station properly equipped to perform those functions and holding–

i) An instrument rating, Class I;

ii) A limited instrument rating appropriate to the make and model of appliance to be tested;

iii) A limited rating appropriate to the test to be performed;

iv) An airframe rating appropriate to the airplane, or helicopter, to be tested; or

3) A certificated mechanic with an airframe rating (static pressure system tests and inspections only).

c) Altimeter and altitude reporting equipment approved under Technical Standard Orders are considered to be tested and inspected as of the date of their manufacture.

d) No person may operate an airplane, or helicopter, in controlled airspace under IFR at an altitude above the maximum altitude at which all altimeters and the automatic altitude reporting system of that airplane, or helicopter, have been tested.

§ 91.413 ATC transponder tests and inspections.

a) No persons may use an ATC transponder that is specified in 91.215(a), 121.345(c), or § 135.143(c) of this chapter unless, within the preceding 24 calendar months, the ATC transponder has been tested and inspected and found to comply with appendix F of part 43 of this chapter; and

b) Following any installation or maintenance on an ATC transponder where data correspondence error could be introduced, the integrated system has been tested, inspected, and found to comply with paragraph (c), appendix E, of part 43 of this chapter.

c) The tests and inspections specified in this section must be conducted by–

1) A certificated repair station properly equipped to perform those functions and holding–

i) A radio rating, Class III;

ii) A limited radio rating appropriate to the make and model transponder to be tested;

iii) A limited rating appropriate to the test to be performed;

2) A holder of a continuous airworthiness maintenance program as provided in part 121 or § 135.411(a)(2) of this chapter; or

3) The manufacturer of the aircraft on which the transponder to be tested is installed, if the transponder was installed by that manufacturer.

Title 14 CFR, Part 119

Certification: Air Carriers and Commercial Operators

§ 119.1 Applicability.

a) This part applies to each person operating or intending to operate civil aircraft–

1) As an air carrier or commercial operator, or both, in air commerce; or

2) When common carriage is not involved, in operations of U.S.-registered civil airplanes with a seat configuration of 20 or more passengers, or a maximum payload capacity of 6,000 pounds or more.

b) *Requirements prescribed by this part.*

c) *Requirements prescribed by this part.*

d) This part does not govern operations conducted under part 91, subpart K (when common carriage is not involved) nor does it govern operations conducted under part 129, 133, 137, or 139 of this chapter.

e) Except for operations when common carriage is not involved conducted with airplanes having a passenger-seat configuration of 20 seats or more, excluding any required crewmember seat, or a payload capacity of 6,000 pounds or more, this part does not apply to–

1) Student instruction;

2) Nonstop Commercial Air Tours conducted after September 11, 2007, in an airplane or helicopter having a standard airworthiness certificate and passenger-seat configuration of 30 seats or fewer and a maximum payload capacity of 7,500 pounds or less that begin and end at the same airport, and are conducted within a 25-statute mile radius of that airport, in compliance with the Letter of Authorization issued under § 91.147 of this chapter.

For nonstop Commercial Air Tours conducted in accordance with part 136, subpart B of this chapter, National Parks Air Tour Management, the requirements of part 119 of this chapter apply unless excepted in § 136.37(g)(2).

For Nonstop Commercial Air Tours conducted in the vicinity of the Grand Canyon National Park, Arizona, the requirements of SFAR 50-2, part 93, subpart U, and part 119 of this chapter, as applicable, apply.

3) Ferry or training flights;

4) Aerial work operations, including–

   i) Crop dusting, seeding, spraying, and bird chasing;

   ii) Banner towing;

   iii) Aerial photography or survey;

   iv) Fire fighting;

   v) *Certain helicopter operations*; and

   vi) Powerline or pipeline patrol;

5) Sightseeing flights conducted in hot air balloons;

6) Nonstop flights conducted within a 25-statute-mile radius of the airport of takeoff carrying persons or objects for the purpose of conducting intentional parachute operations.

7) *Certain helicopter flights.*

8) *Part 133 operations.*

9) Emergency mail service conducted under 49 U.S.C. 41906;

10) Operations conducted under the provisions of § 91.321 of this chapter; or

11) *Small UAS operations conducted under part 107 of this chapter.*

Title 14 CFR, Part 135

Operating Requirements: Commuter and On Demand Operations and Rules Governing Persons on Board Such Aircraft

§ 135.243 Pilot in command qualifications.

a) No certificate holder may use a person, nor may any person serve, as pilot in command in passenger-carrying operations–

1) Of a turbojet airplane, of an airplane having a passenger-seat configuration, excluding each crewmember seat, of 10 seats or more, or of a multiengine airplane in a commuter operation as defined in part 119 of this chapter, unless that person holds an airline transport pilot certificate with appropriate category and class ratings and, if required, an appropriate type rating for that airplane.

2) *Helicopter operations.*

b) Except as provided in paragraph (a) of this section, no certificate holder may use a person, nor may any person serve, as pilot in command of an aircraft under VFR unless that person–

1) Holds at least a commercial pilot certificate with appropriate category and class ratings and, if required, an appropriate type rating for that aircraft; and

2) Has had at least 500 hours time as a pilot, including at least 100 hours of cross-country flight time, at least 25 hours of which were at night; and

3) For an airplane, holds an instrument rating or an airline transport pilot certificate with an airplane category rating; or

4) *Helicopter operations.*

c) Except as provided in paragraph (a) of this section, no certificate holder may use a person, nor may any person serve, as pilot in command of an aircraft under IFR unless that person–

1) Holds at least a commercial pilot certificate with appropriate category and class ratings and, if required, an appropriate type rating for that aircraft; and

2) Has had at least 1,200 hours of flight time as a pilot, including 500 hours of cross country flight time, 100 hours of night flight time, and

75 hours of actual or simulated instrument time at least 50 hours of which were in actual flight; and

3) For an airplane, holds an instrument rating or an airline transport pilot certificate with an airplane category rating; or

4) *Helicopter operations.*

d) Paragraph (b)(3) of this section does not apply when–

1) The aircraft used is a single reciprocating-engine-powered airplane;

2) The certificate holder does not conduct any operation pursuant to a published flight schedule which specifies five or more round trips a week between two or more points and places between which the round trips are performed, and does not transport mail by air under a contract or contracts with the United States Postal Service having total amount estimated at the beginning of any semiannual reporting period (January 1-June 30; July 1-December 31) to be in excess of $20,000 over the 12 months commencing with the beginning of the reporting period;

3) The area, as specified in the certificate holder's operations specifications, is an isolated area, as determined by the Flight Standards office, if it is shown that–

i) The primary means of navigation in the area is by pilotage, since radio navigational aids are largely ineffective; and

ii) The primary means of transportation in the area is by air;

4) Each flight is conducted under day VFR with a ceiling of not less than 1,000 feet and visibility not less than 3 statute miles;

5) Weather reports or forecasts, or any combination of them, indicate that for the period commencing with the planned departure and ending 30 minutes after the planned arrival at the destination the flight may be conducted under VFR with a ceiling of not less than 1,000 feet and visibility of not less than 3 statute miles, except that if weather reports and forecasts are not available, the pilot in command may use that pilot's observations or those of other persons competent to

supply weather observations if those observations indicate the flight may be conducted under VFR with the ceiling and visibility required in this paragraph;

6) The distance of each flight from the certificate holder's base of operation to destination does not exceed 250 nautical miles for a pilot who holds a commercial pilot certificate with an airplane rating without an instrument rating, provided the pilot's certificate does not contain any limitation to the contrary; and

7) The areas to be flown are approved by the responsible Flight Standards office and are listed in the certificate holder's operations specifications.

§ 135.267 Flight time limitations and rest requirements: Unscheduled one- and two-pilot crews.

a) No certificate holder may assign any flight crewmember, and no flight crewmember may accept an assignment, for flight time as a member of a one- or two-pilot crew if that crewmember's total flight time in all commercial flying will exceed–

1) 500 hours in any calendar quarter.

2) 800 hours in any two consecutive calendar quarters.

3) 1,400 hours in any calendar year.

b) Except as provided in paragraph (c) of this section, during any 24 consecutive hours the total flight time of the assigned flight when added to any other commercial flying by that flight crewmember may not exceed-

1) 8 hours for a flight crew consisting of one pilot; or

2) 10 hours for a flight crew consisting of two pilots qualified under this part for the operation being conducted.

c) A flight crewmember's flight time may exceed the flight time limits of paragraph (b) of this section if the assigned flight time occurs during a regularly assigned duty period of no more than 14 hours and–

1) If this duty period is immediately preceded by and followed by a required rest period of at least 10 consecutive hours of rest;

2) If flight time is assigned during this period, that total flight time when added to any other commercial flying by the flight crewmember may not exceed–

   i) 8 hours for a flight crew consisting of one pilot; or

   ii) 10 hours for a flight crew consisting of two pilots; and

3) If the combined duty and rest periods equal 24 hours.

d) Each assignment under paragraph (b) of this section must provide for at least 10 consecutive hours of rest during the 24-hour period that precedes the planned completion time of the assignment.

e) When a flight crewmember has exceeded the daily flight time limitations in this section, because of circumstances beyond the control of the certificate holder or flight crewmember (such as adverse weather conditions), that flight crewmember must have a rest period before being assigned or accepting an assignment for flight time of at least–

   1) 11 consecutive hours of rest if the flight time limitation is exceeded by not more than 30 minutes;

   2) 12 consecutive hours of rest if the flight time limitation is exceeded by more than 30 minutes, but not more than 60 minutes; and

   3) 16 consecutive hours of rest if the flight time limitation is exceeded by more than 60 minutes.

f) The certificate holder must provide each flight crewmember at least 13 rest periods of at least 24 consecutive hours each in each calendar quarter.

Title 14 CFR, Part 141

Pilot Schools

Appendix D to Part 141–Commercial Pilot Certification Course

1. Applicability. This appendix prescribes the minimum curriculum for a commercial pilot certification course required under this part, for the following ratings:

a) Airplane single-engine.

b) Airplane multiengine.

c) *Rotorcraft helicopter*.

d) *Rotorcraft gyroplane*.

e) *Powered-lift*.

f) *Glider*.

g) *Lighter-than-air airship*.

h) *Lighter-than-air balloon*.

2. Eligibility for enrollment. A person must hold the following prior to enrolling in the flight portion of the commercial pilot certification course:

a) At least a private pilot certificate; and

b) If the course is for a rating in an airplane or a powered-lift category, then the person must:

1) Hold an instrument rating in the aircraft that is appropriate to the aircraft category rating for which the course applies; or

2) Be concurrently enrolled in an instrument rating course that is appropriate to the aircraft category rating for which the course applies, and pass the required instrument rating practical test prior to completing the commercial pilot certification course.

3. Aeronautical knowledge training.

a) Each approved course must include at least the following ground training on the aeronautical knowledge areas listed in paragraph (b) of this section, appropriate to the aircraft category and class rating for which the course applies:

1) **35 hours of training** if the course is for an airplane category rating or a powered-lift category rating.

2) *Lighter-than-air airship.*

3) *Rotorcraft.*

4) *Glider.*

5) *Lighter-than-air balloon.*

b) Ground training must include the following aeronautical knowledge areas:

1) Federal Aviation Regulations that apply to commercial pilot privileges, limitations, and flight operations;

2) Accident reporting requirements of the National Transportation Safety Board;

3) Basic aerodynamics and the principles of flight;

4) Meteorology, to include recognition of critical weather situations, windshear recognition and avoidance, and the use of aeronautical weather reports and forecasts;

5) Safe and efficient operation of aircraft;

6) Weight and balance computations;

7) Use of performance charts;

8) Significance and effects of exceeding aircraft performance limitations;

9) Use of aeronautical charts and a magnetic compass for pilotage and dead reckoning;

10) Use of air navigation facilities;

11) Aeronautical decision making and judgment;

12) Principles and functions of aircraft systems;

13) Maneuvers, procedures, and emergency operations appropriate to the aircraft;

14) Night and high-altitude operations;

15) Descriptions of and procedures for operating within the National Airspace System; and

16) Procedures for flight and ground training for lighter-than-air ratings.

4. Flight training.

a) Each approved course must include at least the following flight training, as provided in this section and section No. 5 of this appendix, on the approved areas of operation listed in paragraph (d) of this section that are appropriate to the aircraft category and class rating for which the course applies:

1) **120 hours of training** if the course is for an airplane or powered-lift rating.

2) *Airship rating.*

3) *Rotorcraft rating.*

4) *Glider rating.*

5) *Balloon rating.*

b) Each approved course must include at least the following flight training:

1) **For an airplane single-engine course**: 55 hours of flight training from a certificated flight instructor on the approved areas of operation listed in paragraph (d)(1) of this section that includes at least–

i) Ten hours of instrument training using a view-limiting device including attitude instrument flying, partial panel skills, recovery from unusual flight attitudes, and intercepting and tracking navigational systems. Five hours of the 10 hours required on instrument training must be in a single engine airplane;

ii) Ten hours of training in a complex airplane, a turbine-powered airplane, or a technically advanced airplane that meets the requirements of § 61.129(j) of this chapter, or any combination thereof. The airplane must be appropriate to land or sea for the rating sought;

iii) One 2-hour cross country flight in daytime conditions in a single engine airplane that consists of a total straight-line distance of more than 100 nautical miles from the original point of departure;

iv) One 2-hour cross country flight in nighttime conditions in a single engine airplane that consists of a total straight-line distance of more than 100 nautical miles from the original point of departure; and

v) 3 hours in a single-engine airplane in preparation for the practical test within 60 days preceding the date of the test.

2) **For an airplane multiengine course**: 55 hours of flight training from a certificated flight instructor on the approved areas of operation listed in paragraph (d)(2) of this section that includes at least–

i) Ten hours of instrument training using a view-limiting device including attitude instrument flying, partial panel skills, recovery from unusual flight attitudes, and intercepting and tracking navigational systems. Five hours of the 10 hours required on instrument training must be in a multiengine airplane;

ii) 10 hours of training in a multiengine complex or turbine-powered airplane, or any combination thereof;

iii) One 2-hour cross country flight in daytime conditions in a multiengine airplane that consists of a total straight-line distance of more than 100 nautical miles from the original point of departure;

iv) One 2-hour cross country flight in nighttime conditions in a multiengine airplane that consists of a total straight-line distance of more than 100 nautical miles from the original point of departure; and

v) 3 hours in a multiengine airplane in preparation for the practical test within 60 days preceding the date of the test.

3) *Rotorcraft helicopter course.*

4) *Rotorcraft gyroplane course.*

5) *Powered-lift course.*

6) *Glider course.*

7) *Lighter-than-air airship course.*

8) *Lighter-than-air balloon course.*

c) For the use of full flight simulators or flight training devices:

1) The course may include training in a full flight simulator or flight training device, provided it is representative of the aircraft for which the course is approved, meets the requirements of this paragraph, and is given by an authorized instructor.

2) Training in a full flight simulator that meets the requirements of § 141.41(a) may be credited for a maximum of 30 percent of the total flight training hour requirements of the approved course, or of this section, whichever is less.

3) Training in a flight training device that meets the requirements of § 141.41(a) may be credited for a maximum of 20 percent of the total flight training hour requirements of the approved course, or of this section, whichever is less.

4) Training in the flight training devices described in paragraphs (c)(2) and (3) of this section, if used in combination, may be credited for a maximum of 30 percent of the total flight training hour requirements of the approved course, or of this section, whichever is less. However, credit for training in a flight training device that meets the requirements of § 141.41(a) cannot exceed the limitation provided for in paragraph (c)(3) of this section.

d) Each approved course must include the flight training on the approved areas of operation listed in this paragraph that are appropriate to the aircraft category and class rating–

1) **For an airplane single-engine course**:

i) Preflight preparation;

ii) Preflight procedures;

iii) Airport and seaplane base operations;

iv) Takeoffs, landings, and go-arounds;

v) Performance maneuvers;

vi) Navigation;

vii) Slow flight and stalls;

viii) Emergency operations;

ix) High-altitude operations; and

x) Postflight procedures.

2) **For an airplane multiengine course**:

i) Preflight preparation;

ii) Preflight procedures;

iii) Airport and seaplane base operations;

iv) Takeoffs, landings, and go-arounds;

v) Performance maneuvers;

vi) Navigation;

vii) Slow flight and stalls;

viii) Emergency operations;

ix) Multiengine operations;

x) High-altitude operations; and

xi) Postflight procedures.

3) *For a rotorcraft helicopter course.*

4) *For a rotorcraft gyroplane course.*

5) *For a powered-lift course.*

6) *For a glider course.*

7) *For a lighter-than-air airship course.*

8) *For a lighter-than-air balloon course.*

5. Solo training. Each approved course must include at least the following solo flight training:

a) **For an airplane single engine course**. Ten hours of solo flight time in a single engine airplane, or 10 hours of flight time while performing the duties of pilot in command in a single engine airplane with an authorized instructor on board. The training must consist of the approved areas of operation under paragraph (d)(1) of section 4 of this appendix, and include–

1) One cross-country flight, if the training is being performed in the State of Hawaii, with landings at a minimum of three points, and one of the segments consisting of a straight-line distance of at least 150 nautical miles;

2) One cross-country flight, if the training is being performed in a State other than Hawaii, with landings at a minimum of three points, and one segment of the flight consisting of a straight-line distance of at least 250 nautical miles; and

3) 5 hours in night VFR conditions with 10 takeoffs and 10 landings (with each landing involving a flight with a traffic pattern) at an airport with an operating control tower.

b) **For an airplane multiengine course**. Ten hours of solo flight time in a multiengine airplane, or 10 hours of flight time while performing the duties of pilot in command in a multiengine airplane with an authorized instructor on board. The training must consist of the approved areas of operation under paragraph (d)(2) of section 4 of this appendix, and in-clude–

1) One cross-country flight, if the training is being performed in the State of Hawaii, with landings at a minimum of three points, and one of the segments consisting of a straight-line distance of at least 150 nautical miles;

2) One cross-country flight, if the training is being performed in a State other than Hawaii, with landings at a minimum of three points and one segment of the flight consisting of straight-line distance of at least 250 nautical miles; and

3) 5 hours in night VFR conditions with 10 takeoffs and 10 landings (with each landing involving a flight with a traffic pattern) at an airport with an operating control tower.

c) *Rotorcraft helicopter course.*

d) *Rotorcraft-gyroplane course.*

e) *Powered-lift course.*

f) *Glider course.*

g) *Lighter-than-air airship course.*

h) *Lighter-than-air balloon course.*

6. Stage checks and end-of-course tests.

a) Each student enrolled in a commercial pilot course must satisfactorily accomplish the stage checks and end-of-course tests, in accordance with the school's approved training course, consisting of the approved areas of operation listed in paragraph (d) of section No. 4 of this appendix that are appropriate to aircraft category and class rating for which the course applies.

b) Each student must demonstrate satisfactory proficiency prior to re-ceiving an endorsement to operate an aircraft in solo flight.

Title 49 CFR, Part 830

Notification and Reporting of Aircraft Accidents or Incidents and Overdue Aircraft, and Preservation of Aircraft Wreckage, Mail, Cargo, and Records

§ 830.2 Definitions.

As used in this part the following words or phrases are defined as follows:

Aircraft accident means an occurrence associated with the operation of an aircraft which takes place between the time any person boards the aircraft with the intention of flight and all such persons have disembarked, and in which any person suffers death or serious injury, or in which the aircraft receives substantial damage. For purposes of this part, the definition of "aircraft accident" includes "unmanned aircraft accident," as defined herein.

Civil aircraft means any aircraft other than a public aircraft.

Fatal injury means any injury which results in death within 30 days of the accident.

Incident means an occurrence other than an accident, associated with the operation of an aircraft, which affects or could affect the safety of operations.

Operator means any person who causes or authorizes the operation of an aircraft, such as the owner, lessee, or bailee of an aircraft.

Public aircraft means an aircraft used only for the United States Government, or an aircraft owned and operated (except for commercial purposes) or exclusively leased for at least 90 continuous days by a government other than the United States Government, including a State, the District of Columbia, a territory or possession of the United States, or a political subdivision of that government. "Public aircraft" does not include a government-owned aircraft transporting property for commercial purposes and does not include a government-owned aircraft transporting passengers other than: transporting (for other than commercial purposes) crewmembers or other persons aboard the aircraft whose presence is required to perform, or is associated with the performance of, a governmental function such as firefighting, search and rescue, law enforcement, aeronautical research, or biological or geological resource management; or transporting (for other than commercial purposes) persons aboard the aircraft if the aircraft is operated by the Armed Forces or an intelligence agency of the United States. Notwithstanding any limitation relating to use of the aircraft for commercial purposes, an aircraft shall be considered to be a public aircraft without regard to whether it is operated by a unit of government on behalf of another unit of government pursuant to a cost reimbursement agreement, if the unit of government on whose behalf the operation is conducted certifies to the Administrator of the Federal Aviation Administration that the operation was necessary to respond to a significant and imminent threat to life or property (including natural resources) and that no service by a private operator was reasonably available to meet the threat.

Serious injury means any injury which: (1) Requires hospitalization for more than 48 hours, commencing within 7 days from the date of the injury was received; (2) results in a fracture of any bone (except simple fractures of fingers, toes, or nose); (3) causes severe hemorrhages, nerve, muscle, or tendon damage; (4) involves any internal organ; or (5) involves second- or third-degree burns, or any burns affecting more than 5 percent of the body surface.

Substantial damage means damage or failure which adversely affects the structural strength, performance, or flight characteristics of the aircraft, and which would normally require major repair or replacement of the affected component. Engine failure or damage limited to an engine if only one engine fails or is damaged, bent fairings or cowling, dented skin, small punctured holes in the skin or fabric, ground damage to rotor or propeller blades, and damage to landing gear, wheels, tires, flaps, engine accessories, brakes, or wingtips are not considered "substantial damage" for the purpose of this part.

Unmanned aircraft accident means an occurrence associated with the operation of any public or civil unmanned aircraft system that takes place between the time that the system is activated with the purpose of flight and the time that the system is deactivated at the conclusion of its mission, in which:

1) Any person suffers death or serious injury; or

2) The aircraft has a maximum gross takeoff weight of 300 pounds or greater and sustains substantial damage.

§ 830.5 Immediate notification.

The operator of any civil aircraft, or any public aircraft not operated by the Armed Forces or an intelligence agency of the United States, or any foreign aircraft shall immediately, and by the most expeditious means available, notify the nearest National Transportation Safety Board (NTSB) office,[1] when:

a) An aircraft accident or any of the following listed serious incidents occur:

   1) Flight control system malfunction or failure;

   2) Inability of any required flight crewmember to perform normal flight duties as a result of injury or illness;

   3) Failure of any internal turbine engine component that results in the escape of debris other than out the exhaust path;

   4) In-flight fire;

   5) Aircraft collision in flight;

   6) Damage to property, other than the aircraft, estimated to exceed $25,000 for repair (including materials and labor) or fair market value in the event of total loss, whichever is less.

   7) For large multiengine aircraft (more than 12,500 pounds maximum certificated takeoff weight):

      i) In-flight failure of electrical systems which requires the sustained use of an emergency bus powered by a back-up source such as a battery, auxiliary power unit, or air-driven generator to retain flight control or essential instruments;

      ii) In-flight failure of hydraulic systems that results in sustained reliance on the sole remaining hydraulic or mechanical system for movement of flight control surfaces;

      iii) Sustained loss of the power or thrust produced by two or more engines; and

iv) An evacuation of an aircraft in which an emergency egress system is utilized.

8) Release of all or a portion of a propeller blade from an aircraft, excluding release caused solely by ground contact;

9) A complete loss of information, excluding flickering, from more than 50 percent of an aircraft's cockpit displays known as:

i) Electronic Flight Instrument System (EFIS) displays;

ii) Engine Indication and Crew Alerting System (EICAS) displays;

iii) Electronic Centralized Aircraft Monitor (ECAM) displays; or

iv) Other displays of this type, which generally include a primary flight display (PFD), primary navigation display (PND), and other integrated displays;

10) Airborne Collision and Avoidance System (ACAS) resolution advisories issued when an aircraft is being operated on an instrument flight rules flight plan and compliance with the advisory is necessary to avert a substantial risk of collision between two or more aircraft.

11) Damage to helicopter tail or main rotor blades, including ground damage, that requires major repair or replacement of the blade(s);

12) Any event in which an operator, when operating an airplane as an air carrier at a public-use airport on land:

i) Lands or departs on a taxiway, incorrect runway, or other area not designed as a runway; or

ii) Experiences a runway incursion that requires the operator or the crew of another aircraft or vehicle to take immediate corrective action to avoid a collision.

b) An aircraft is overdue and is believed to have been involved in an accident.

Supplemental Excerpts

Sourced from Legal Interpretations and Advisory Circulars

U.S. Department
of Transportation

**Federal Aviation
Administration**

B. Dan Crowe FEB -4 2013
Palm Beach Helicopters
2615 Lantana Rd.
Lantana, FL 33462

Dear Mr. Crowe:

This letter responds to your request for legal interpretation dated September 26, 2012. You
have indicated that you currently hold a commercial pilot certificate with an airplane
category single engine land rating. You have asked several questions pertaining to adding a
rotorcraft category helicopter class rating to your commercial pilot certificate.

A person who adds a category rating to a pilot certificate must, among other things,
complete the training and the applicable aeronautical experience for the category of aircraft.
14 C.F.R. § 61.63(b)(1). To apply for a rotorcraft category helicopter class rating at the
commercial pilot certificate level, a pilot must accomplish 100 hours of pilot-in-command
flight time, which includes at least 35 hours in helicopters. 14 C.F.R. §61.129(c)(2). The
pilot must also complete 10 hours of solo flight time in a helicopter or 10 hours of flight
time performing the duties of pilot in command in a helicopter with an authorized instructor
on board. 14 C.F.R. § 61.129(c)(4). Section 61.129(c)(4) states that a pilot may credit the 10
hours of solo flight time or 10 hours of flight time performing the duties of pilot in
command with an authorized instructor on board toward the pilot in command flight time
required by § 61.129(c)(2).

You have asked the following questions:

**May the applicant credit more than 10 hours of time spent performing the duties of
pilot in command with an instructor on board toward the PIC requirements of §
61.129(c)(2)? May the applicant log as PIC time that time spent performing the duties
of pilot in command with an instructor on board in accordance with § 61.51?**

Section 61.129(c)(4) permits a pilot to credit a maximum of 10 hours of flight time
performing the duties of pilot in command with an instructor on board toward the pilot-in-
command flight time required by § 61.129(c)(2). As such, the remaining 25 hours of pilot-
in-command flight time in helicopters required by § 61.129(c)(2) must meet the pilot-in-
command logging requirements in § 61.51(e).

Under § 61.51(e)(1), a pilot may log pilot-in-command flight time when the pilot (i) is the sole manipulator of the controls of an aircraft for which the pilot is rated (category, class, and type rating, if appropriate), (ii) is the sole occupant of an aircraft, or (iii) acts as PIC of an aircraft for which more than one pilot is required under the type certification of the aircraft or the regulations under which the flight is conducted.[1] Additionally, in 2009, the FAA introduced another avenue through which a pilot could log pilot-in-command flight time. 74 FR 42500, Aug. 21, 2009. Section 61.51(e)(1)(iv) permits a pilot who holds a commercial pilot certificate or airline transport pilot certificate that is appropriate to category and class of aircraft to log pilot-in-command flight time while performing "the duties of pilot in command while under the supervision of a qualified pilot in command" if, among other things, the pilot is undergoing an approved PIC training program. Legal Interpretation to John Duncan (April 13, 2012).

Because you are adding a rotorcraft category helicopter class rating to a commercial pilot certificate without holding a rotorcraft category helicopter class rating at the private pilot certificate level, you are not able to log pilot-in-command flight time under § 61.51(e)(1)(i), (iii), or (iv) because those provisions require a pilot to be rated in the aircraft. Because you do not hold the appropriate category and class rating, the only provision under which you may log the remaining pilot-in-command flight time is as the sole occupant of the aircraft.

Does the applicant need an endorsement under § 61.31 in order to perform the duties of pilot in command with an instructor on board in accordance with § 61.129(c)(4)?

Under § 61.31(d), to act as the pilot in command of an aircraft, a person must: (1) hold the appropriate category, class, and type rating (if a class or type rating is required) for the aircraft to be flown; or (2) have received training required by part 61 that is appropriate to the pilot certification level, aircraft category, class, and type rating (if a class or type rating is required) for the aircraft to be flown, and have received an endorsement for solo flight in that aircraft from an authorized instructor.

A pilot who is "performing the duties of pilot in command" under the supervision of another pilot – in this case an authorized flight instructor – is not acting as pilot in command of the aircraft during solo flight and, therefore, does not need an endorsement under § 61.31(d). A pilot requires a § 61.31(d) endorsement only for the purpose of conducting solo flight in an aircraft for which the pilot is not rated.

May an applicant who has been endorsed for solo flight under § 61.31 credit or log a portion of the flight training conducted in accordance with § 61.129(c)(3) as PIC time after receiving such an endorsement?

Section 61.31(d) sets forth the requirements for acting as pilot in command of an aircraft. An endorsement for solo flight under that section does not alter the requirements for logging

---

[1] Under 14 C.F.R. § 1.1, a pilot in command must hold the appropriate category, class, and type rating for the conduct of the flight. Additionally, under § 61.31(d), to serve as pilot in command of an aircraft, a person must hold the appropriate category, class, and type rating (if required) for the aircraft to be flown unless conducting a solo flight under an instructor endorsement.

pilot-in-command flight time under § 61.51(e). As such, notwithstanding the 10 hours of flight time that may be credited under §61.129(c)(4), a pilot who holds a § 61.31(d) endorsement for solo flight may not log or credit flight training with an authorized instructor as pilot-in-command flight time because the pilot is neither rated in the aircraft nor the sole occupant of the aircraft.

This response was prepared by Anne Moore, an attorney in the International Law, Legislation, and Regulations Division of the Office of the Chief Counsel, and has been coordinated with the Airman Certification and Training Branch of Flight Standards Service. If you have any additional questions regarding this matter, please contact us at your convenience at (202) 267-3073.

Sincerely,

Mark W. Bury
Acting Assistant Chief Counsel for International Law,
Legislation, and Regulations Division, AGC-200

U.S. Department
of Transportation

**Federal Aviation
Administration**

Advisory
Circular

Subject: PRIVATE CARRIAGE VERSUS COMMON	Date: **4/24/86**	AC No: **120-12A**
CARRIAGE OF PERSONS OR PROPERTY	Initiated by: AFS-820	Change:

---

1. PURPOSE. This advisory circular furnishes Federal Aviation Administration (FAA) personnel and interested segments of industry with general guidelines for determining whether current or proposed transportation operations by air constitute private or common carriage. If the operations are in interstate or foreign commerce, this distinction determines whether or not the operator needs economic authority as an "air carrier" from the Department of Transportation. Operations that constitute common carriage are required to be conducted under Federal Aviation Regulations (FAR) Parts 121 or 135. Private carriage may be conducted under FAR Parts 125 or 91, Subpart D. Operations conducted under FAR Section 91.181, which permits certain charges to be made, may also be subject to these guidelines , particularly the "time sharing" provisions of FAR Section 91.181(c)(1). It should also be noted that lease agreements entered into under FAR Section 91.181 are subject to FAR Section 91.54, "Truth in leasing clause requirement in leases and conditional sales contracts."

2. CANCELLATION. Advisory Circular 120-12, Private Carriage Versus Common Carriage By Commercial Operators Using Large Aircraft, dated June 24, 1964, is canceled.

3 BACKGROUND. "Common carriage" and "private carriage" are common law terms. The Federal Aviation Act of 1958 uses the term "common carriage" but does not define it. It has therefore been determined that guidelines giving general explanations of the term "common carriage" and its opposite, "private carriage," would be helpful,

4. GUIDELINES. A carrier becomes a common carrier when it "holds itself out" to the public, or to a segment of the public, as willing to furnish transportation within the limits of its facilities to any person who wants it. Absence of tariffs or rate schedules, transportation only pursuant to separately negotiated contracts, or occasional refusals to transport, are not conclusive proof that the carrier is not a common carrier. There are four elements in defining a common carrier; (1) a holding out of a willingness to (2) transport persons or property (3) from place to place (4) for compensation. This "holding out" which makes a person a common carrier can be done in many ways and it does not matter how it is done.

    a. Signs and advertising are the most direct means of "holding out" but are not the only ones.

b. A "holding **out**" may be accomplished through the actions of agents, agencies, or salesmen who may, themselves, procure passenger traffic from the general public and collect them into groups to be carried by the operator. It is particularly important to determine if such agents or salesmen are in the business of selling transportation to the traveling public not only through the **"group"** approach but also by individual ticketing on known common carriers.

c. **Physicall**y holding out without advertising where a reputation to serve all is gained is sufficient to constitute an offer to carry all customers. There are many means by which physical holding out may take place. For example, the expression of willingness to all customers **with whom** contact is made that the operator can and will perform the requested service is sufficient. The fact that the holding out generates little success is of no consequence. The nature and character of the operation are the important issue.

d. Carriage for hire which does not involve "holding **out**" is private carriage. Private carriers for hire are sometimes called "contract carriers," but the term is borrowed from the Interstate Commerce Act and legally inaccurate when used in connection with the Federal Aviation Act. Private carriage for hire is carriage for one or several selected customers, generally on a long-term basis. The number of contracts must not be too great, otherwise it implies a willingness to make a contract with anybody. A carrier operating pursuant to **18** to **24** contracts has been held to be a common carrier because it held itself out to **serve** the public generally to the extent of its facilities. Private **carriage has been** found in cases where three contracts have been the sole basis of the operator's business. Special adaptation of the transportation service to the individual needs of shippers is a factor tending to establish private carriage but is not necessarily conclusive.

e. A carrier holding itself out as generally willing to carry only certain kinds of traffic is, nevertheless, a common carrier. For instance, a carrier authorized or willing only to carry planeloads of passengers, cargo, or mail on a charter basis is a common carrier, if it so holds itself out. This is, in fact, the basic business of supplemental air carriers.

f. A carrier flying charters for only one organization may be a common carrier if membership in the organization and participation in the flights are, in effect, open to a significant segment of the public. Similarly, a carrier which flies planeload charters for a common carrier, carrying the latter's traffic, engages in common carriage itself.

g. Occasionally, offers of free transportation have been made to the general public by hotels, casinos, etc. In such cases, nominal charges have been made which, according to the operators, bear the expense of gifts and gratuities. However, the operators maintain that the transportation is free. The courts have held that such operations are common carriage based on the fact that the passengers are drawn from the general public and the nominal charge constituted compensation.

h. Persons admittedly operating as common carriers in a certain field (for instance, in intrastate commerce) sometimes claim that transportation for hire which they perform in other fields (for instance, interstate or foreign commerce) is private carriage. To sustain such a claim, the carrier must show that the private carriage is clearly distinguishable from its common carriage business and outside the scope of its holding out. The claimed private carriage must be viewed in relation to and against the background of the entire carrying activity. Historically, Civil Aeronautics Board decisions have concluded that only in rare instances could carriage engaged in by a common carrier be legitimately classified as private.

i. In summary, persons intending to conduct only private operations in support of other business should look cautiously at any proposal for **revenue-**generating flights which most likely would require certification as an air carrier.

j. Persons **who** have questions concerning intended operation of their aircraft are encouraged to discuss their proposed operation with the Regional Counsel of the FAA region in which it intends to establish its principal business office. Such early interviews will materially assist the applicant in avoiding many of the "pitfalls" which could result in illegal common carriage operations.

William T. Brennan
Acting Director of Flight Standards

Benjamin (Ben) Samples

Ben grew up around aviation and holds an airline transport pilot certificate and a gold-seal flight instructor certificate in airplanes and helicopters. He has served as a chief flight instructor and professor with a university Part 141 flight school and as a check airman with a Part 141 helicopter school (with examining authority). He worked with the West Virginia Department of Aviation and has conducted flight training for the West Virginia State Police.

Ben served with the United States Army and the West Virginia National Guard in the 19th SFG(A) and is a co-founder of Patch Aero. He completed bachelor's degrees from West Virginia University in Aerospace and Mechanical Engineering, a master's degree from Mountain State University in IDS Quality Management and Engineering Technologies, a master's degree from the University of Washington in Human Centered Design and Engineering, and is currently completing his dissertation at the Union Institute & University on ethical/creative approaches to aviation training and reducing the LOC-I problem.

Casey Rice

Casey has been working in aviation for the last 17 years. He started his career with the United States Army, serving as an Apache helicopter mechanic with the 82nd Airborne. He holds an airline transport pilot certificate, is type rated on the Airbus A320 transport category aircraft, is a gold seal flight instructor in airplanes and helicopters, and is also an airframe and powerplant mechanic.

Casey is a co-founder of Patch Aero. He has served as a Part 133 and Part 135 chief and is currently a chief flight instructor with a Part 141 airplane flight school while completing his Inspector Authorization (IA). He previously served as a chief flight instructor with a Part 141 helicopter school (with examining authority). Casey is also experienced in night vision goggle operations and vertical-reference/longline operations.

Ben and Casey first collaborated around 2014 when Casey taught Ben to fly helicopters and Ben taught Casey to fly airplanes. They have been challenging each other ever since. They are both FAASTeam Representatives with the FAA. They have owned two airplanes together and provided tailwheel instruction for several years out of Lantana Airport in Lake Worth, FL. The two have also developed/delivered Part 61 and Part 141 training course outlines (TCO).

PATCH AERO

The Patch Mission
Our mission is to equip aviators in their continual pursuit of excellence.

The Patch Vision
We envision an aviation renaissance, where pilots exemplify lifelong learning and elevate the ideal we foster as aviators. We believe lifelong learning is both an individual and collaborative activity, where new experiences continually refine our skills and knowledge toward a safer and more perfect paradigm. We believe aviation's reputation hinges on mentoring, encouraging, and challenging one another as a community of aviators.